The Good Alliance

Feminism, Religion, and Education

Denise Lardner Carmody
The University of Tulsa

UNIVERSITY
PRESS OF
AMERICA

Lanham • New York • London

Copyright © 1991 by
University Press of America®, Inc.
4720 Boston Way
Lanham, Maryland 20706

3 Henrietta Street
London WC2E 8LU England

Library of Congress Cataloging-in-Publication Data

Carmody, Denise Lardner, 1935-
The good alliance : feminism, religion, and education /
Denise Lardner Carmody.
p.   cm.
1. Feminism—Religious aspects—Catholic Church.   2. Women in
Christianity.   3. Theology—Study and teaching—United States.
4. Religion—Study and teaching—United States.   5. Education,
Higher—Aims and objectives.   6. Catholic Church—Doctrines.
7. United States—Church history—20th century.   I. Title.
BX1795.F44C37   1991
291'.071'173—dc20   90–49380 CIP

ISBN 0–8191–8044–0 (alk. paper)
ISBN 0–8191–8045–9 (pbk.: alk. paper)

For Richard and Beverly Prosser Gelwick

Contents

Preface

In reviewing the public lectures that I have been asked to give recently, I have found that three themes stand out: feminism, religion, and education. These have been the major preoccupations of the people who have invited me to their campuses or professional meetings, and I have been happy to reflect on all three, because all three shape my professional and personal life. This volume presents some of the work to which such invitations have led, as well as some further reflections on the relations among feminism, religion, and education. The general argument that the book presents is that it is good for feminism, religion, and education to think of themselves as allies.

It is a pleasant task to thank my husband, John Carmody, for his collaboration on several of the lectures that became raw material for chapters here. As well, I should express my appreciation to the audiences at Maryville College, at the 1989 College Theology Society's Pre-Convention Workshop, at St. Scholastica's College, at the College of Notre Dame of Maryland, at Pittsburgh State University (Kansas), and at the Section on the Academic Teaching and Study of Religion at the 1989 American Academy of Religion's Annual Convention for their attention, challenging questions, and supportive responses. All of these audiences have strengthened my convictions about the good alliance that feminists, believers, and educators can fashion, and all have buoyed my hopes that sexism, superficiality, and ignorance need not have the last word.

Finally, I wish to express my gratitude to the Warren Center for Catholic Studies at The University of Tulsa for support in publishing this book.

I

INTRODUCTION

A teacher strives to make connection. Central to education is the effort to help people see how their worlds--natural, social, and personal--hang together. One of the loudest complaints about higher education nowadays is that so many curricula lack coherence. Students pass through a smorgasbord of courses but regularly come away malnourished. So those of us teaching in the humanities now tend to be especially sensitive to the questions of coherence and nourishment. On the one hand, we have to face the fact that graduate training still tends to favor specialization more than generalization. On the other hand, we have to find responsible ways of accommodating (ideally, fostering) interdisciplinary approaches that bring out the connections among ranges of data wide and deep enough to illumine problems of real significance to the lives of ordinary people.

Women's studies and religious studies, two relative newcomers to the curricula of many American colleges, have been generous contributors to the campaign for coherence and interdisciplinarity. On the whole, scholars in both areas have found it natural, if not imperative, to draw on a variety of disciplinary viewpoints. Thus, historical, philosophical, sociological, literary, and other methods crisscross both women's studies and religious studies. Because most of the problems under investigation have sharp existential implications, scholars in both women's studies and religious studies tend to distrust a single disciplinary viewpoint. One might say that because the existential implications are sharp, the surgeons want to see the target area in the round, as a hologram.

1

Moreover, the feminist approaches that have emerged in women's studies have sometimes joined (and sometimes clashed with) approaches to studying religious phenomena. While some feminists continue to castigate religion as a bastion of sexism, others have stressed the strengths that many women have drawn from their cultures' deepest intuitions about the ultimate structures and goals of human existence. From the side of religious studies, some scholars continue to regard feminism as a fad (and some theologians continue to regard it as heretical), but many other scholars find religious experience--that of men as well as women-- illumined considerably by feminist theory. As a matter of current practice, then, there is a significant overlap between feminist scholarship, much of which occurs in the context of academic women's studies programs, and scholarship focused on religion. In reviewing my own teaching and lecturing in recent years, I have found this overlap to be spreading. Rather naturally, therefore, I have begun to think about an alliance between feminism and religion.

The third player in the game that we consider in this book is education. By "education" I shall usually mean what goes on in college classrooms, in possible distinction from what goes on in grammar school, high school, or graduate (university) classrooms. My focus on the classroom is not meant to neglect or depreciate what goes on in libraries and other places where scholarly research develops, but it is meant to stress the practical side of the educational venture. I certainly believe that scholarly research is crucial to the mission of higher education, and I agree with those who argue that good college teaching benefits greatly from ongoing research and publication. But in some institutions of higher education students tend to be pushed from the center of concern. Professors can feel torn between what they owe the students in their courses and what is going to forward their standing among their peers. Professors and administrators alike can focus their evaluations of faculty on scholarly publication so sharply that they broadcast loud and clear the message that teaching is at best a negative control: bad teaching will harm your prospects for advancement, but good teaching will run a distant second to scholarly publication when it comes to tenure and promotion. Without getting into the complicated relationship between this outlook and the recent failures of American higher education to graduate a truly literate, competent citizenry, I want to assume that college teachers should be committed to academic publication and concentrate here on what they do with and for students.

One of the things that courses in women's studies and religious studies tend to do for students is raise their consciousness of the complexity of many problems and so of the need for interdisciplinary approaches. Another thing is to provide a stimulus and forum for the discussion of values, worldviews, and ultimate meanings. Feminist approaches that question the sexual alignments that have prevailed in the past raise profound questions about what sexuality means, about how perceptions of sex color the world of work, about what influence they have on economic arrangements, and the like. After the dawn of feminist awareness, no sector of a culture is immune to a profound reevaluation. Education, medicine, the arts, the sciences, religion, politics--name your poison and feminists will both deepen your sense of its toxicity and suggest an antidote.

The same can be true of courses in religious studies. Once students have seen that how people think about the ultimate construction and destiny of the world is crucial to their sense of what is possible in either public or private life, such students begin to look at any culture--Irish, Israeli, Iranian, or Indian--with a new eye. The complexity of current events in Northern Ireland, along the West Bank of the Jordan River, in Tehran and New Delhi becomes in part a function of the Protestant, Catholic, Jewish, Muslim, or Hindu senses of reality (both actual reality and ideal reality) that pulsate in those places.

The injustices that galvanize feminists bring into many college classrooms a concrete exemplification of the thesis that our prejudgments about other people greatly affect our treatment of them. As well, they concretize the obverse side of that thesis: what we experience other people to be shapes our sense of their reality, their value, and their place in the overall scheme of things.

The appreciations of mystery that the religious studies courses I most admire bring into the classroom can be similarly explosive. Once students have realized that the wisdoms most revered throughout history have usually included a strong confession of human finitude, they are likely to take the student newspaper, and even the New York Times, down a peg. Religious studies help students appreciate the dazzling variety of rituals, myths, doctrines, and social forms that human beings have created to deal with the mysteriousness of their lives. Equally significantly, however, religious studies can help students attend to such bedrock facts as their own mortality, their inevitable ignorance of things they would dearly like to know, and their own sinfulness. These are what some philosophers call "existentials:" permanent factors shaping every human situation. A college that did not attend to them would leave its students horribly ill-equipped for their most significant spiritual struggles and so very poorly educated.

By now, the drift of my reflections should be plain. I want to illustrate ways in which the raised consciousness that courses in women's studies, religious studies, and other fields that take sex and divine mystery seriously can educate students for a truly beautiful, profound, realistic, and satisfying life. Without denying that higher education has some obligation to help students earn their bread and sustain their physical existence, my overriding interest is what people who work in higher education have to offer when it comes to spiritual existence--questions of meaning, value, destiny. I am interested in the foundations of a truly humane existence. The humanity that I want to educe in my students centers in what people think in times of crisis, or times of ecstasy, or times of desolation, or times of special creativity. The argument that I am weaving through the chapters presented here is that feminism, religion, and higher education ought to be allies in the work of interpreting such crucial times so that students, and many others, can appreciate the real choices confronting them. With Deuteronomy, I believe that there are two ways, of death and of life, and that we should do all we can to help people choose life. Because I find feminism, religion, and education great sources of encouragement to choose life, I want to yoke them together as helpmates.

The Logic of this Book

The first topic that we deal with, feminist consciousness and world peace, forces us to begin

4

concretely. The stereotype is that women prefer the concrete to the abstract, and the personal to the impersonal, so I hope that this beginning proves especially congenial to women's interests. My treatment of women's usual response to war and violence begins with a recent novel but it soon becomes religious. As noted, some feminists despise religion, because they consider it part of the patriarchal history that has abused many women. But I distinguish between the institutional and cultural effects of the world's religions and the human need to ponder ultimate questions. This human need has led many women and men to the contemplative life, the life that tries to appreciate human existence as a whole and honor its mysteriousness. Inasmuch as such contemplation is tied up with much of our best art, philosophy, and commonsensical wisdom, it seems to me highly desirable. Indeed, when I come across doctrinaire atheism or antagonism to religion I feel myself to be in the presence of something woefully immature. Without the depth that religious contemplation gives it, our abhorrence of warfare and other senseless abuses of human flesh would not measure up to the giant obstacles we face on the way to peace.

On the academic side of the relationship between feminism and religion stand recent efforts to integrate feminist perspectives into the courses of religious studies departments. Inasmuch as the courses that departments offer are the skeleton of any college's curriculum, such efforts carry several implications for liberal education as a whole. My own convictions about the rightness of revising departmental course offerings to reflect the impact of feminist perspectives derive from three sources. I have found that students need these perspectives, that providing them is a matter of justice (rendering the female half of the human race its due), and that teachers wanting to be faithful to God have to take seriously the religious implications of such justice.

From the impact that feminist perspectives ought to be making on course offerings in religious studies we move to a topic that correlates feminism and religion from the other side, religion's natural center in questions about the character of divinity or ultimate reality. Under the spur of feminism, many theologians have begun to reconsider their language about God. Inasmuch as biblical language rests on the assumption that human beings are images of the divine, theologians trying to understand the God revealed in the Bible have to take seriously the significance of feminine experience and feminine imagery for God. By reflecting on such traditionally masculine traits as God's control of history, such stereotypically feminine traits as God's care for human beings, and on the practical implications of giving feminine imagery for the divine some parity with masculine imagery, I try to show both women's full portion in the divine nature and the truly mysterious character of the God worthy of worship.

The majority of women have worshiped in churches, temples, mosques, and other houses of prayer. The majority of women have been children of their given culture and so members of the religious bodies developed in their given culture to mediate their contacts with divinity. To specify the implications of this general state of affairs for the religious context most pertinent for most of my readers, I take up the question of women's experience in the Christian church. Here my beginning is autobiographical: a review of some of the high points, and low points, of my own often intense involvement with the Roman Catholic church. Then I move to reflections on some of the role models that Christian history, both past and recent, offers to women of today. Last I discuss developments in women's senses of Christian faith and church membership suggested by the work of recent leading feminist theologians.

The story of women's experience in the Christian church has been an ambiguous tale, full of both good things and bad. So has the story of the overall impact that the world religions have made on their adherents, male and female alike. In moving to this broader story, I hope to broaden the consideration of what religion has been and now ought to strive to become. This consideration has links to my prior consideration of women's typical approaches to world peace, so I begin with references to the context one needs if one is to estimate the significance of a religious leader such as the Ayatollah Khomeini or Pope John-Paul II. Then I reflect on the tragic fact that Islam, Christianity, and many other religions have often been sources of militant hatred and destruction. Finally, I consider the role that religion ought to play in mental health, showing both the destructive implications of

6

religious claims to chosenness and the need to make divinity truly transcendent of human sinfulness.

Chapters 2 through 6 therefore illustrate rather concretely how feminist and religious interests overlap in the work of a professor like me, who feels committed to both perspectives. Chapters 7-9 assume such an overlap and concentrate on educational questions. First, I deal with the quite topical issue of values in the curriculum of the typical liberal arts college. This issue has become topical because many would-be reformers of American college education have charged that students are not receiving a proper exposure to their Western heritage, including the values on which (the reformers claim) the United States was built. Without getting into the history of American higher education, I try to build some bridges to secular professors and articulate a view of curricular values that stresses the admirations that students ought to be developing. Thus, I speak about the wonder that natural science, social science, the humanities, and theological studies ought to inculcate. As well, I speak about how teachers in the different disciplines might alert their students to the opportunities for growth in self-knowledge that each curricular area offers. Throughout, I find that developing critical intelligence and compassion (virtues traditionally stereotyped as male and female) is the goal I would want college teachers to target.

Against this general background, I turn next to the question of values in honors education: what teachers might do for their best and brightest. Here the further nuances that emerge include a more refined sense of how the disciplinary areas (natural sciences, social sciences, humanities) correlate and a more ambitious sense of how students may be stimulated toward genuine intellectualism. By way of illustrating creativity in the development of core curricula for good students, I present some proposals of Thomas Berry for an education centered on what we presently know about the history and needs of the earth. Then I present what I hope are strong arguments for the intellectual freedom that creative academic work requires.

Having looked at curricular matters in some detail, I conclude my educational studies somewhat personally. For years I have defined myself as a college teacher, and on the occasion of being invited to give the outstanding teacher lecture at the 1989 Annual Meeting of the Academy of Religion I found myself digging into the roots of what admirable college teaching requires. What is the authority by which one professes to lead students into the mysteries of divinity and humanity? What are the main responsibilities that the teaching profession lays upon us? The religious character of my efforts to answer these questions perhaps shows that one cannot outrun the thoughts of one's masters, while the personal form of my reflections owes many debts to feminine mistresses I have admired.

In concluding, I have tried to step back from the particulars of the different chapters and reflect again on the relations among feminism, religion, and education. The result has been a strengthening of my conviction that religion is the substance of an authentic human life and that feminism and education can be wonderful modes of expressing this substance and sharing it.

FEMINIST CONSCIOUSNESS AND WORLD PEACE

Zoe Coleman, the heroine of Mary Morris's fine novel <u>The Waiting Room</u> (New York: Doubleday, 1989), has a healing touch. After wandering through several different countries and jobs, she falls into work at a clinic for the very poor in Brazil. There she discovers that she is good with the sick, able to help and console them. So she returns to the United States, enters medical school, and plans on a career in medicine. Her future would be bright, except that her past has been blighted by war. Her father came back from the Second World War morose and deranged. The man she loved from high school days was killed in Vietnam. Her brother, the person to whom she has the greatest emotional ties, came home crazy from exile in Canada, where he had fled to escape Vietnam. At the core of Morris's novel, then, lies the antagonism between healing and warfare. Indeed, Morris puts at the head of her work a quotation from Marguerite Duras's book <u>The War</u>: "We are the only ones who are still waiting, in a suspense as old as time, that of women, everywhere, waiting for the men to come home from the war."

Women wait for men to come home from war. The waiting room is their lives, the container of their time. Zoe Coleman's grandmother fled from Cossacks whose sport was killing Jewish children. The one man the grandmother loved was killed by gangsters the day before their wedding. Zoe's mother waited for her husband to come home from the Second World War, and then waited for his spirit to return to his body. It never did. War and violence have laid the lives of all the Coleman women to waste. And, if Duras is correct, the Colemans simply repeat millennial patterns, begun in that time out of mind when men began to specialize in killing and women in nurturing and healing. From these millennial patterns, the majority of women today have an instinctive hatred of war. War, we believe, is the magnification of senselessness that most threatens our souls.

When one is alerted to this age-old lament, Rachel weeping for children because they are no more, women's sufferings from war begin to appear everywhere. In an essay published in the editorial pages of the New York Times for December 21, 1989, Susan Cohen commemorated the first anniversary of the crash of Pan Am Flight 103 in Lockerbie, Scotland. Her daughter, her only child, a student at Syracuse University, died in that crash, an innocent victim of terrorism. Cohen suggests that ever since she herself has been only partly living: "I haven't recovered. I never will. I cry much of the time. I who never before took anything stronger than an aspirin now take anti-depressants and anti-anxiety drugs every day, shored up by therapists. The loss of a beloved child is the worst loss in the world. Theo was my future, and now I have no future. Theo's youth kept me young. Now I'm old."

Need I remind you that Pan Am Flight 103 was destroyed by Muslim terrorists trying to avenge the deaths of Iranians shot down by Americans in the Persian Gulf? Need I remind you that men are the vast majority of such terrorists, as they are the vast majority of the sailors who man warships, and the generals who command troops, and the politicians who give the generals their go-ahead? No doubt women have always puzzled over the connection between men and violence, men and terrorism, men and children lost horribly, but recently women have begun to articulate their puzzlement more pointedly. For example, among the people interviewed after a man went crazy in Montreal in the late Fall of 1989 and killed dozens of women was a middle-aged woman who kept muttering, to herself more than the interviewers, "Why is it always men who do the killing?" Even if one could point to female terrorists, or women who went on a rampage at a grammar school and shot little children, this question would remain. Why have men been the butchers of history? Why have the Hitlers and Stalins and Maos who have done the grossest slaughterings been men?

10

It follows that feminist consciousness is likely to approach a topic such as world peace with anger and bias and deep sorrow. I myself once had four brothers. Now I have three, courtesy of the Battle of the Bulge and General Patton. I had not realized the depth of my anger until the movie about Patton starring George C. Scott brought the General back into public discussion. No matter how many people tell me that the Second World War was necessary, or that the General was a military genius, Patton will always be my enemy, the man who got my brother Tommy killed. Men who are committed to war, who are professional killers, are the enemies of women. Overall, women are made by biology or socialization to bring forth life and nurture it. Women are made to be mothers, teachers, healers. No proper sophistication about women's equality with men in professional potential, brains, virtue, or vice negates this reality. Violence and war and death are caused by men much more than by women. So the men who support the military cultures, who think the thoughts and make the machines that keep the world in its cycles of warfare and hatred, are the deadly enemies of most women, whether those women realize it or not.

Some aspects of the battle between the sexes may be humorous, even romantic, but this aspect is not. I believe that if women ran the world, violence and unnecessary death would be cut at least in half. I believe that a major reason why feminist consciousness is a moral imperative is that without feminist consciousness the forces of sanity are hopelessly crippled. Until the great majority of human beings come to the conviction that the killing power of men and the life-creating power of women are not on a par, we shall continue to have the dualism that makes women wait for men to come home from war. So I believe that stereotypically feminine instincts and virtues light the way for the survival of our species. Let me devote the rest of this chapter to explaining this belief.

The Causes of War

Wars begin for many different reasons, but high among the causes of most wars is a sense of injustice, real or contrived. People fight because they don't like one another, and they don't like one another because they perceive one another as threats. In the past, or the present, or the future that we imagine, the other group threatens to take away something that we hold precious or may subject us to a suffering that we consider outrageous. That suffering can be physical: the wounds of battle, or the pains of poverty. It can be spiritual: humiliation, shame, self-hatred.

More often than not, the trigger of war is more spiritual than physical. The terrorists responsible for the crash of Pan Am Flight 103 had not themselves crashed in the downing of the Iranian jetliner. Their thirst for revenge was ideological, part of the mad religion that sees insult everywhere and makes people think they can become the scourge of God. Most of warfare, historically, has stemmed from such ideology. If people's physical needs or ambitions played a role, their hatreds and sense of wounded pride were much more significant. That remains true today. American troops finally invaded Panama because President Bush was tired of feeling that General Noriega was thumbing his nose at the United States. The leaders of Communist China turned on their own youth and massacred them in Beijing because they felt the youth threatened their power. In Africa, in Afghanistan, in Northern Ireland, in the Middle East, in the violence of the death throes of Communism in Eastern Europe, in Latin America, and just about everywhere else poverty is important but hatred and pride are the more important causes of war. War is a sign of spiritual disease. It is stimulated by suffering bodies, and it expresses itself in bodily blows, but its deepest roots lie in people's minds and hearts, where the desolations of godlessness moan and howl.

I know, you may tell me that the worst wars are religious--that there is no hatred like that pitting god against god. You may even tell me that the female deities created by religions can drip with blood and spotlight death. The Great Goddess of prehistoric Europe brings forth life throughout nature, but she also presides over death. The Great Goddess of millennial India assumes the terrible incarnation of Kali, who comes garlanded with skulls. Nonetheless, I still reply that the religion responsible for the mental disease of war is nothing holy, and nothing formed by the full contribution of women that any holy religion would welcome. For while women hate those who rape them, who kill their children, or who humiliate their tribe, women also learn to tolerate ambivalence, to doubt black and white dichotomies, to specialize in the reconciliations necessary if children are to be

12

socialized, if communities are to fashion their networks of information and help, if men are to be calmed toward the sanity that calculates before it builds its towers or rolls out its guns.

It is possible, of course, that women put in charge of the world would find that warfare is necessary. It is possible that with power comes the compulsion to subjugate others, or a wisdom that thinks it necessary to destroy villages in order to save them. The greater probability that I see, however, is that women put in charge of the world would form circles in which problems threatening to incite violence could be talked out and so defused. The greater probability that I see is that war would not be women's prevailing reflex or accomplishment. To be sure, women and the world they ruled would have other problems, because women have other sins and deficiencies. But the world would not be so close to nuclear disaster, and the religious hatreds so ominous at the flash points around the globe would be counterbalanced by a vivid sense of what happens to flesh when guns fire at it, or bombs blow it apart, or knives rip into it.

Are there things for which people ought to be prepared to die? No doubt there are, but few of them show up in the United Nations, or in the councils of the super-powers, or in the war rooms of the NATO forces or the Warsaw Pact. People ought to be prepared to die because cancer can overwhelm them, or because earthquakes can topple buildings upon them, or because cars or planes can fail, or because drug addicts or psychopaths can forget their humanity. People should not have to be prepared to die because male bloodlust requires regular expression, or because egomaniacal dictators need sacrifices like Moloch, or because nations are so stupid that they will trade thousands of mangled bodies for a few miles of wretched territory, or because generals and military contractors don't know how or have no will to shut down the machinery of war. People should not have to be prepared to die because their leaders are so cynical that they will not listen to Socrates, or Jesus, or the Buddha, or the Mahatma Gandhi and make spiritual goods the pearls of great price. People, all of us, deserve better than the leaders most countries elect or have forced upon them. It is irrational, and cowardly, and stupid in the extreme to settle for brutality and loss as we so regularly do. It is an insult to place a heart beat

13

away from the highest office in our land a callow jingoist such as J. Danforth Quayle--an insult that any sane electorate would have turned against George Bush to smash his candidacy to smithereens. Alas, women often participate in such insanity, such contradiction of their own manifest best interest. The causes of war are the causes of our general political dementia. They lie so deep in our souls that nothing less than divinity can eradicate them.

Peace and Grace

When theologians talk about sin, the profound irrationality that nothing less than divinity can eradicate, they generally encounter squirms or yawns. We don't like to confront sin, because such a confrontation implies our need for conversion--changing our ways and making a new start. We profess to be bored with sin because we won't see that sin is exactly what is giving us so much pain. We experience our job to be warped, part of a system that we cannot respect. That is sin. We experience our extended family to be crazy and self-destructive, as though bedeviled by a mad genie. That is sin. We don't love ourselves, and we don't think that anyone else really could. That is sin. We see pictures of homeless people, and then we read about a new government giveaway that will send tens of millions of dollars abroad, or about a new government scandal that has wasted billions. The absurd juxtaposition of the two is sin: culpably wrong irrationality. In my state, which ranks 48th in support for education, children are mortgaged to the egos of lawmakers and the niggardliness of the general electorate. Second graders appear with their teachers on television begging for basic supplies: pencils, crayons, paper, textbooks. Unless kind viewers donate such supplies, the classrooms go unstocked. That is sin, made only the uglier by the cant of Bible-belters against the secular humanism they think has invaded public education.

When he viewed the caverns of human sin, the apostle Paul realized why the Son of God had to die. Under the symbolism of Adam's fall stood such a wholesale alienation from reason and love (from God), that humanity itself had become impotent. Unhappy people that we were, who would rescue us from the bondage of sin and death? The nearly incredible good news was and is that Paul had an answer for that

14

terrible question: the grace of God; the love poured forth in our hearts by the Holy Spirit in virtue of the death and resurrection of Christ.

I have to say that I have less and less patience with feminists who deride the death and resurrection of Christ, or language about sin and grace, or references to the peace that surpasses human understanding. I have to say that feminist consciousness antagonistic to religious wisdom strikes me as incredibly half-baked. Whether in the context of polemics about abortion, or in academic ventures in feminist theory, the ignorance of sin and grace that prevails in many feminist circles is like Kierkegaard's sickness unto death. If there is one thing certain, it is suffering and death caused by human folly and malice. If there is one thing necessary, it is salvation from human folly and malice. To ignore these bedrock certainties, or fail to translate them into better language (if one's complaint is that they sound medieval) is to be puerile--a masculine adjective for a childishness that applies to too many feminists.

Where such puerility applies, one will find little peace, either personal or aimed at the wide world. World peace gleams in prospect as a function of human maturity. The time may come when, by accepting the overtures of God, people agree to share the resources of the earth rather than kill one another over them. The time may come when pride and honor mean less than doing what is right, protecting the future of little children, loving the flesh that is God's precious gift to us. Many men long for such a time, but more women can feel how it would be shaped. It would be shaped by people's thinking about their lives as amazing gifts and opportunities. It would come like the caress of a mothering love, gentle and soothing, able to hush the demons that say we have to grab and dominate.

There is no obscurity about the clues to the eschaton, the time when God would be all in all and peace would proclaim God's presence. The clues lie in our own souls, as down payments on heaven that we can turn a profit on right now. Peace, St. Augustine said, is the tranquillity of order. Order, the philosopher Eric Voegelin made plain, is a function of consciousness--of becoming aware of how the Beginning and the Beyond that frame our intellectual light define our reality. We have no humanity apart from this

15

Beginning and Beyond. Without the mysteries of where we came from and where we are going, we would not be the unique species we are. As Martin Heidegger put it, Man *fragt*: We are the species that raises questions. To be sure, neither Augustine, nor Voegelin, nor Heidegger developed a theory of consciousness fully adequate for today's feminists. But all three were so much more profound than the puerile secularists I mentioned above that thinking their thoughts after them is a pure pleasure. For each, the order revealed to the realistic is a function of something mysterious. We only become attuned to the way things really are when we are willing and able to contemplate the Beginning and the Beyond.

Without contemplation, Scripture says, the people perish. All over the world, people are perishing today, in both battle and mindless busyness, because they are not contemplative. To be contemplative is to think with a calm concentration that naturally becomes holistic. It is to be moved by the most enjoyable feelings of one's soul to prefer the whole to the partial, the common good to the private pleasure. What makes this activity congenial is the sense it brings that one has been made to think in this way: globally, relationally, ecologically, mystically. Peace of soul is a function of contemplative love. Certainly, it is only healthy when it moves into and out from action to improve the world and forward social justice, but in itself peace of soul depends upon what Aquinas called "complacency": taking pleasure in being with the whole, the divinity that is more intimate to us than we are to ourselves. As long as feminists, or any other contemporary group, do not balance their activist concern with a contemplative complacency, they will be stumbling blocks to world peace.

Feminist Holism

It is a truism among many feminists that women's genius runs toward relatedness, connectedness, giving and receiving in ways that make for communion and community. Women are keenly aware of nuance, implication, subtle signs of felt meaning. If this window onto the connectedness of natural and social reality as a whole often threatens to make women confused and indecisive, that is a small price to pay for the richness it discloses. Life itself is interlocking, interwoven, in ways that we neglect to

16

our peril. If the ecological crisis shows us anything, it is how simple-minded, how puerile, our mechanistic or rectilinear models of nature have been. The same logic applies to much of our social and political thinking. We have blinded ourselves to the connections among poverty, sexism, racism, crime, drugs, economic disparities, the military-industrial complex, and the limits of nature. We have chosen to ignore the shamans, prophets, and sages who have insisted that we not put asunder what God joined together in creation-- who have insisted that we must reflect, meditate, and pray if we are to know what sort of world we inhabit. Our problem is not a lack of solid traditional wisdom about how to deal with the world. Our problem is our ignorance of this tradition and the cowardice that keeps us from testing it. Most of us would rather flee from self-knowledge than examine our consciences each night. Most of us don't want to know the things for our peace. So the figure of Jesus weeping over Jerusalem keeps coming to mind. The irony, ultimately happy, is that losing our lives to find the things for our peace is a nearly pure pleasure. When we start to contemplate, to accept holism, to open our hearts to the love that causes the Beginning and the Beyond to frame our awareness, we start to become free. The cant and self-delusion quiet down. We can hear ourselves think, and below our own thoughts we can hear the call of God's Spirit, who moves in our depths with sighs too deep for words to make the prayer that pleases God.

Many women know this prayer very well. Many women have entered a church, lighted a candle, and let the darkness embrace them like a tender sister. As the tears ran down their cheeks, they have poured out their pains to God, or to the Mother of Christ, or simply to the silence that was so much better than the storm of accusations they had fled. Certainly, many men have done this also, and in maturity women and men differ very little in their ability to let thought and feeling flow together. Yet the stereotype is that praying in church is women's work, and so the stereotype is that the darkness, the quiet, the scent and flicker of the candles offer nothing of real significance. The feminist consciousness that I want to promote believes the exact opposite.

For a truly holistic feminism, the buoyant force on every side is the mystery of God, present as She chooses to be, with us all days, even unto the consummation of the world in joy and peace. And this divine presence is our guide to peace-making. The eschaton is not merely an act of grace, coming from the domain of God that we call heaven to take our world beyond where it could go by itself. The eschaton is also in our midst, working right now, like the measure of leaven that makes the bread rise. The parables of Jesus about the Kingdom of God stress this immanence. With the coming of Christ, salvation has been accomplished. At root, God has done everything that needed to be done, resecuring creation and history in the divine goodness. So Paul spoke of Christ as the Second Adam and the New Creation. So the rising we celebrate at Easter is the rebirth of all good human possibilities. Right now, if we wish, we can touch and feel the love that is the gist of the eschaton. Right now the Spirit of Christ labors to spread the peace and joy tokening the divine goodness. Naturally, one only appreciates such possibilities in faith, which is God's gift. Still, any people who contemplate the real needs of humanity are primed to receive God's gift. For any people who contemplate the real needs of humanity sense, in their bones, that only a love stronger than evil and death could put us right. That was Christ's exact message and way.

Peace and Christ's Way

To conclude these reflections, which have turned out to be radically Christian, let me place before you some feminist variations on the traditional Christian wisdom that God's way of saving the world has been to embrace our evils in a much stronger love. If we take seriously the most basic symbolism in Christian art, the cross of Christ, we realize the truth of Isaiah's intuition: As far as the heavens are above the earth, so are God's ways above our human ways. God's way was to take the sufferings that ravage human existence and make them the medium of a new creation. God's way was to overcome the malice, the deadly evil symbolized by "Satan," by sending a champion who could let Satan do his worst. As Dostoevski's Grand Inquisitor appreciated, most people have not been willing to accept God's way of salvation. The freedom that God's way demands, as the condition of an exhaustive, truly passionate love, has proven too much for most of us. So we have ceded our birthright for a mess of pottage and let dictators and fools run our lives. We have tolerated stupidity in high places and trash on what should have been high ways to peace because we have had eyes but would not see, have had ears but would not hear. What could be more plain than the crucified Christ hanging over the altar as the epitome of God's wisdom? How much more elementary could God have made the message? The cross shows what the world, the human mentality that does not want to know the things for its peace, does to the messengers of God. That is where his life of healing and teaching and witnessing to his Father's love took Jesus of Nazareth. And yet that is where God triumphed, overcoming the world. Do we believe this bald Christian gospel? Is it the wisdom on which we have staked our lives? Or are we not really believers?

I find the question embarrassing. It tears apart my pretensions to Christian faith and shows how much I am an unbeliever. Yet by the grace of God even such embarrassment can be salutary. At least I am reminded why so many of my ideas and works turn out to be impotent. At least I glimpse once again what an adequate praxis of peace might entail.

An adequate praxis of peace might entail a profound rejection of all the false gods that my culture lays out for my worship. It might put in their wretched place the money, and the pleasure, and the fine clothes, and the exotic travel, and even the esteem of my peers that the advertisers tout as the great tokens of success. What makes for peace is not money or status or power. It is goodness--virtue, in the sense of the strength that comes from being stabilized by God's love. Jesus was so good that neither the seductions of Satan nor the threats of the religious authorities who judged Jesus to be their mortal enemy had much impact upon him. The key to the life of Jesus is the love of his Father that defined his very personality. So strong was this love, so completely did it give Jesus his identity, that from earliest Christian times the followers of Jesus realized that Jesus was completely the child of divinity. As the child of divinity, Jesus was defined by something immortal. The living God is deathless, athanatos, and so Jesus was deathless. The resurrection revealed how fully divinity had taken Jesus to itself. It could not be that death would conquer Jesus because Jesus was what divinity itself was. So the peace that Jesus breathed upon his disciples was the peace of divinity. The Holy Spirit bequeathed by the resurrected Christ is the breath of God that takes people to the divine love that caused the world to come to be and so is free of the world's corruptions. Yet all of this became manifest only through Jesus's passage along the way of the Cross. By the inscrutable counsels of God, all of it depended on the willingness of the vulnerable man Jesus to accept the worst that human beings could do and surrender his spirit into God's keeping.

The feminist consciousness that I most admire is both fierce with a love of life fanned through millennia of bringing forth children and willing to stand by the cross of Christ and receive his body for its final anointing. Even though most of the men had fled, the women stayed faithful to the end, letting their spirits be pierced with each blow of the hammer. And when it had been consummated, the women trudged forth to do more women's work--preparing the body for burial. What a rich and painful symbolism: in most traditional cultures the sex that brings forth life prepares the body for burial. In the worst of cases, like that of Mary the Mother of Jesus, the body to be prepared is the woman's own child. My sense is that if we put at the conference tables that decide matters of war and peace some women who had held in their arms their own dead children, war would become a minor problem.

The wisdoms that we need to make world peace are the wisdoms of the cross and the sundered human body. It is the disembodied minds, the ideological ranters, who impose wars upon us. People who love life, who have names like Zoe, who know the beauty and frailty of the human body because they have wrapped it in swaddling clothes, or bathed it in sickrooms, or prepared it for burial, are nearly bound to reject warfare as virulently inhuman. At the antipodes from the prophets of war, those who would glorify war as the rite of passage to manhood, they insist that because God made us as we are, vulnerable and mortal through and through, we ought to outlaw war and all the other ways of blaspheming against human flesh. The argument of Shakespeare's Shylock was that if you pricked him he would bleed. He was one with the bigots who despised him for his Jewishness because he and they shared the same kind of flesh.

20

Christians, who are unique among all the religionists of the world for the enfleshed character of their deity, ought to be the world's foremost pacifists. If they knew even the abcs of their own faith, they would realize that the cross of their God is not only the sign of his paradoxical triumph but also the sign of divine judgment against human violence. And of course the Christians to whom I look for the quickest assimilation of this catechism are the women who have dealt most intimately with human flesh. Surely they ought to lead the cause of protecting life against the follies of those who would endanger it by machismo. Surely they ought to be the most eloquent about the wonders of God's gift of life, from conception to final burial. Our lives, the enfleshment of God's image in us, are too sacred to be wasted on the expediencies of war. The feminist peacemaking I most admire is passionately convinced of that.

III

INTEGRATING FEMINIST PERSPECTIVES
INTO THE RELIGIOUS STUDIES CURRICULUM

My interest here is to set the question of why it is important to represent women's voices by integrating feminist perspectives into the religious studies curriculum. In reflecting on this question, I have realized that one cannot separate it from the question of how such an integration might take place, so my essay will inevitably make some practical suggestions. Nonetheless, I think it valuable to ruminate about the end, the telos, of integrating feminist perspectives into the religious studies as a question useful in its own right. My rumination has three sub-topics: students' needs, intellectual justice, and fidelity to God.

1. Students' Needs

Recently I taught two of my typical courses: "Women and World Religions" and "The New Testament and Literature." Both courses are part of the Tulsa Curriculum, our general education sequence. Each course had about 30 students, but only two of those in "Women and World Religions" were men, while "The New Testament and Literature" had about 15 men. It is hard to say, though, which sex needed feminist perspectives more.

In my part of the country, "feminism" is an ambiguous term. Evangelical religion mingles with a southern form of the national pursuit of affluence to set much of the agenda for the social self. Being a woman is often supposed to mean being a lady, and being a lady is often idealized as having a Bible in one hand and five figures' worth of diamonds on the other. To bring forward perspectives that would challenge the notions of humanity and maturity tacit in such a combination of images is to trim one's sails for heavy weather. Still, I believe that exploring the radical implications of either sexual equality or Christian faith is very good work--precisely the sort that lured me and many of my friends into teaching religious studies. My students, and I assume students generally, need both better information and exercises that improve their ability to analyze such information, synthesize their diverse studies, and communicate their judgments effectively. More profoundly, however, they need challenges to the worldviews implied in the mass media and many Sunday sermons. More profoundly, they need visions of what it means to be fully human, holy, precisely as sexed beings. Inalienably, we are all members of a two-sexed species. Great portions of our creativity and peace depend on our loving this fate. I see the integration of feminist perspectives into the religious studies curriculum as a small but potent way of helping the next generation find such a love.

A decade ago, the better female students I had at Penn State and Wichita State were generally enthusiastic about feminism. They felt that Gloria Steinem and Marlo Thomas were speaking for them. Five years ago I was meeting many female students who thought sexual discrimination was a thing of the past. Their boyfriends were attentive and they expected the job market to be welcoming. Now matters seem more complex. Date rape, an experience of 10 percent of the respondents to a survey at my campus, has stirred some female students to examine sexual relations more deeply. The louder volume of the controversies about abortion has stirred others. And the awful question of sexually transmitted diseases has threatened to scar the entire student body. Looking at the students from my geriatric status, I sometimes feel heartsick with compassion. On the one hand, I push them harder and harder on the academic side, giving ever lower grades, it seems, because their laziness infuriates me. On the other hand, the more I learn about their personal circumstances--the divorces in their homes, the abuses they have suffered, the financial crunch many are in-- the more I realize that being a professor means being forced into the muck of salvation. So many of my students feel soiled, or are in pain, or find it hard to be hopeful about the future that I cannot separate education from healing.

My students need light, vision, the way they need food and love. If the religion that they study with me has great potential for supplying such light, the repression and sexism it has housed threaten to put salvation under a bushel. From one angle, then, stressing feminist perspectives in our religious studies curriculum has meant refining what "religion" ought to denote. More and more, I find myself stressing the wholeness of the religious enterprise. If spirituality is the personal core, politics and theology should not be far behind. If what the churches, synagogues, mosques, and other organizations say and do is significant, so is the mysticism and work for social justice one finds among the unchurched, the religiously disaffected.

What I find hardest to abide in my students, male and female alike, is the unwillingness to <u>think</u> that their religious culture frequently has encouraged in them. It is not just that they assume they know about Jesus, because they have been to Sunday school and heard some bible stories. It is that their God has never become part of their minds. They know about the God who is the consoler of the broken-hearted, and some of them know about the God who himself was broken. Few speak about God herself being moved from the womb, and fewer still think that God is the light of their minds, the ground of their judgment, the context of their universe.

I was thinking about parallels with my students when I read a story in the <u>New York Times</u> (May 14, 1989, page 1) about the growth of evangelical Christianity among traditionally Roman Catholic Hispanics. God knows, Hispanics have numerous reasons for criticizing the way both North and South American Catholicism has treated them. Yet in reading the story I felt a familiar sadness. The evangelical religion so strong in my part of the country is intellectual suicide. It lobotomizes the brain. It has no respectable intellectual tradition and no desire to establish one. Even when it is not smarmy and hypocritical, it gives me the willies, because it falls so far short of the God who would be all in all. Too many of my students not only have never been outside our country but also have no strong desire to visit

Europe, Asia, Africa, or Latin America. Too many not only have no taste for art, ballet, or the symphony but also cannot see why computers and business don't constitute an adequate range of intellectual interests. More often than not, their evangelical religion, or their genial secularism, supports such narrowness. They don't associate either Christianity or Americanness with catholicity--interest in the whole, conviction that nothing human is foreign.

In the matter of gender, my students still tend to consider masculine experience normative and feminine experience ancillary. I have as much difficulty getting female students to use nonsexist language as male students. Naturally, however, it is the male students who have to reach farther if they are to develop a catholic understanding of human nature as both bisexual and transsexual. The females know in their bodies and social psyches that estrogen and subordination are powerful forces. With them the task is placing such forces in historical and philosophical or theological context. With the male students, immaturity is as much a problem as ignorance and lack of sympathy. Too few of my male students show the fascination with being female that one would expect their phase of the lifecycle to engender. Too few want to explore how the world looks to female intelligence, how the world feels to female sensibility. The general culture in which they move makes them complacent about masculine predominance, while their sexual insecurity makes them fear venturing into friendship, serious intellectual as well as emotional communication, with women. They aren't sure what it means to be men, let alone how women share a humanity coeval with maleness and femaleness. So they are happiest when they find women equally uninclined to explore these matters, and the cycle of stereotypes and unreflective thinking continues.

My ventures in courses such as "Women and World Religions" and "The New Testament and Literature" therefore have a mildly prophetic flavor. I have found it counterproductive to be fully explicit about this, but whenever I can underscore the limitations imported by patriarchal thinking in the past or sexual stereotypes of the present, I warm to the opportunity. All the major religious traditions furnish examples of women being shortchanged intellectually and socially. Again and again one finds strong pressures to circumscribe women to the domestic sphere. This should give us pause and help us upgrade the dignity of the domestic sphere, making it something more attractive than what gets hymned on Mothers' Day. But it should also remind us how much our students need to envision women redefining the possibilities of being human by being teachers, doctors, attorneys, artists, diplomats, entrepreneurs. Even when women have gained good access to such professions, they have seldom had the chance to share equally in the remolding of their profession necessary for it to fulfill its humanistic potential.

Higher education is a good example. We are far from the day when a radical sexual equality would have clarified the full heritage that our foremothers and forefathers might be passing on to us and the full sense of humanity that our current potential might set atop national and international agendas. We remain pygmies, captives of the little minds of leaders such as Bush and Quayle, in good measure because our schools and churches have done such a poor job. The crying need of the students I face is for the contemplation without which, Scripture says, the people perish. That is a major reason why integrating feminist perspectives into the religious studies curriculum is a holy work.

2. Intellectual Justice

The second reason why I find feminist perspectives imperative concerns intellectual justice. If we are to represent the past as it was, we have to deal with the past experience of the female half of the human race. If we are to represent the ways that human consciousness reaches out to God, we have to deal with the reaches of women as well as men. This is simply a matter of intellectual honesty or justice. Studies professing to be humanistic, to bear on the experience and makeup of our species, are hopelessly distorted unless they provide for women's voice. Equally, unregenerate courses are a significant part of our educational problem, because they perpetuate the biases and so deformations that have caused both sexes so much pain in the past.

In my usage, then, integrating feminist perspectives into the religious studies curriculum is a matter of giving reality, both past and present, its due. What we are doing when we attempt to upgrade or correct our curricula is responding to a justice both

27

ever ancient and ever new. From the beginning, when Genesis has it that God made the divine image male and female, the dialectical experience of women and men has pressed for acknowledgement. On the one hand, women and men are the same: structured by flesh, reason, and love. On the other hand, women and men are always different bodily and are frequently different in how they perceive and love. This dialectical situation echoes down the pages of history. As well, it continues today. No one knows how to correlate exactly the experiences of women and men, how to arrange the communication that would map the zones that overlap and the zones that diverge. It is not something one can photograph, computerize, or even express in poetry.

This so obvious fact is probably a major blessing, because it reminds even the most obtuse of us that being human is not a patent proposition or project. Our significant definitions are perilous and fraught with mystery. We have to choose who we become, in the process taking a stand on who we are. We have to struggle all our lives to integrate the feedback our sexual roles give us, so that by our end we have made our womanhood or manhood graceful. Yet nothing is more crucial than discovering and producing our humanity, what God has made us. So nothing is more important in our educational ventures than clarifying what we can of the venture that each of us finally has to accomplish for her or himself.

Let me again bend the topic back toward actual students sitting in classrooms and professors' offices. Simply by being a woman in a predominantly male faculty, my presence on several campuses has contributed a tiny dose of intellectual justice. Such a dose is minimal, yet numerous students, mainly females but also a few males, have remarked upon it. Women have to get into the corps of those who fashion curricula and discourse upon the human condition. As a matter of intellectual justice, some people with somatically female experience have to represent what being human in the roles of daughters, sisters, wives, mothers, and the other permutations of femaleness may mean. This is not to say that men cannot or should not concern themselves with these topics, any more than it is to say that women cannot or should not concern themselves with masculine humanity. It is simply to note a brute fact and make it bear on our discussion: the formation of any curricula, those in religious studies or those in other fields bearing on the experiences that shape human beings, ought to include the contributions of women.

Second, it is a matter of intellectual justice to make our curricula at least suggest how the treatment of women and men at the hands of religion has varied through the ages. The word "varied" has two senses here. I mean both how images and ideas have shifted from age to age and how they have distinguished the roles, natures, symbols, and virtues of women from those of men. Religion is substantially what religion does. For female humanity, religion has done some things differently from what it has done for male humanity. Representing these differences is an elementary part of intellectual justice, of fidelity to reality. Now that our consciousness has been alerted to the underside of history, the tendency of reportage and interpretation of the past to neglect feminine humanity, we have no excuse if our discourses on religion do not include how the general edicts and ideas got changed, adapted, or muffled when it came to women. For example, not to indicate in at least sketchy fashion the different consequences that the creation account has had for women and men would be to fail to render intellectual justice.

To be sure, one can encounter analogous arguments from racial or ethnic minorities and so wonder if Pandora isn't raising the lid. But, in my view, the primary differentiation of human beings is sexual, so the first provision for variety and specification ought to be sexual. Ideally we would also note the impact of class, race, age, ethnicity, and other factors, but I believe that sex ought to come first. In both historical and philosophical studies, those wanting to see human nature in the round, with a fully catholic perspective, usually have first to follow Abigail Adams's advice and not forget the ladies.

A third approach to understanding the task of making our religious studies curricula reflect what we know to be required for intellectual justice concerns the variety among women themselves. Each woman has been unique, as well as a being formed by social assumptions and expectations about female humanity. As much as men, women have brought color and change to their roles and the understanding of their sex. If this has not always been apparent, because women often have not been so vociferous as men about their right to be individuals, it has nonetheless been fully real.

For example, the saints we should bring forward for our students as illustrations of Muslim or Christian achievement of female humanity vary considerably. Rabi'a would never be mistaken for Fatima. Monica and Teresa of Avila differ in more than chronology. A truly feminist perspective honors this diversity. It is no enemy of all the further notations one would want to make, after one had limned the main features of most women's religious experience in a given tradition or age, with a given dogmatic or moral teaching. How to hold the many and one together of course is an overarching problem. In my own courses, which tend to be first and second level undergraduate ventures, I am constantly moving back and forth between the general patterns that I believe it my first duty to impart and the exceptions, the variations, I know must be indicated if the course is not to be simpleminded. So whatever those forming curricula can do to provide for case studies in actual religious women's lives will be a great boon. The richer the stories we choose to tell about both women and men, the more likely we are to impart the riches of the reality.

Last, I take it to be a matter of intellectual justice to represent the tangledness of the sexes' views of one another and relate this to their religious tradition's equivalent of original sin. Dorothy Dinnerstein's figure of the mermaid and the minotaur captures the complicity of men and women in the deformations arising from sexism. The accommodations that ladies have exacted from gentlemen and gentlemen have used to pacify ladies are terribly knotted and humorous. The steel magnolia is one easily recognized result, but virtually every culture and mythology has had its equivalent. How else does one explain the imagery of fierce Kali sitting atop an Indian culture whose most prestigious lawgiver, Manu, wanted complete docility from women? How else does one account for the sanctioned shrewishness in the general profile of the traditional Chinese wife and mother? As a matter of rendering reality its due, we have to study the ways that their mutual fear and sin have twisted both women and men, avoiding the bastardized feminism that would make women solely innocent victims.

On every level--historical, psychological,

sociological, theological--women have been actors and reactors, having a substantial say in what the relations between the sexes have been. More subtly, perhaps, women have been interpreters and reformers of the religious traditions, especially in their education of children but also in their many other social roles. I do not mean to say that women's covert power has been the equal of men's overt, politically predominant power. I am not accusing women of a 50 percent share in the blame for our bad laws and bad theology. But I am saying that in the more complex matter of cultural acceptance--how laws and doctrines actually take hold in homes and places of work--women have made a 50 percent contribution, because in this more complex matter agreement and docility, as well as rejection or reinterpretation, are as important as imposition. We have to find ways of making our curricula illumine the religious roots and implications of this tragic, funny, complicated, colorful fact of human history and nature. All of it has to be correlated with release from karmic bondage or salvation from pervasive sin, if we are to display the full power of what the religions have meant by liberation and salvation.

3. Fidelity to God

The third reason why I support efforts to integrate feminist perspectives into the religious studies curriculum stems from faith. One could say that in trying to render intellectual justice people are obeying the call of conscience which is our primary vocation from God, but I want to say something more. The God who appears in the monotheistic religions makes justice a revealed imperative. Sticking to the Christian case, for the sake of simplicity and autobiographical honesty, I find that accounting women as fully human as men is part of the good news of Jesus's kingdom. The too many centuries that it has taken for this realization to become apparent remind us of the power of human sin, but apparent it is for feminists today. Not to make the liberation of women implicit in Jesus's good news an integral part of one's courses on Christianity would be to overlook or conceal something quite central. Just as the beatitudes of Jesus bless the poor, the demeanor of Jesus blesses the women so often considered second class citizens in both his society and many later societies claiming his sanction. The countercultural thrust of the Kingdom of Jesus's God is a permanent feature of the Christian

31

kerygma, because of the permanent opposition between the grace of God and human sin. If we are to be faithful in rendering the import of the Christian gospel, we have to include the liberation Jesus has offered women and the abridgements of that liberation that people not filled with Jesus's Spirit have attempted. Sadly, therefore, we have to deal with the unchristian character of much history in women's regard and the opposition that has often arisen between the Spirit of Christ and church officials.

In my experience, a feminist perspective on Christianity, seeking to understand both the freedom for which Christ has set women free and the enslavements contradicting this freedom, makes plain the hierarchy of truths that ought to govern the Christian's moral life. Paul Tillich expressed much of this notion by discoursing on the "Protestant Principle" that insists on the priority of God in all matters. Catholics have their own tradition of the primacy of existential conscience, embattled though it be, and following feminine perspectives on church membership is a fine way to vivify that tradition. Bluntly put, when feminists find a conflict between the freedom of God that considers women as fully human as men and laws or policies that deny this freedom, they have both the right and the responsibility to follow God's call to freedom. Naturally those serious about their faith will not take the task of discerning such a call of God lightly. Naturally they will try to hear what apparently contrary instructions from those with the charisms of church authority are saying. But in the final crunch none of us can alienate conscience and act heteronomously, least of all those of us who find the very possibility of our faith tied to our God's not being sexist.

It would seem that Vatican II understood this principle when it expressed the episcopal mind about religious liberty, just as it would seem that Vatican II's "Decree on Ecumenism" established once and for all the notion of a hierarchy of truths and so the impossibility of a magisterial positivism that would make any Roman edict a matter of defined faith. But we live in a strange time, when right wing revisionism can seem drunk on the will to power, so it is necessary to reaffirm such elementary matters as each person's need to appropriate the gospel and enjoy the freedom to live out what the Spirit gives her or him to understand the gospel to imply. If feminists find themselves leading the charge in defense of elementary Christian freedom, so much the better. When the dignity of 50 percent of the human race is at issue, one is happy to be found on the side of Christ's angels.

Fidelity to God of course is no license to abuse what has been taught or believed in the past and so create a left-wing revisionism drunk on new wine. For example, I believe that conservatives have a valid complaint when they castigate teachers who represent theses of liberation theology as the clear doctrine of the gospels and tradition. We should own up to the sexism and other limitations of both Scripture and tradition, even as we try to make the case that the better instincts of Jesus or the saints were getting buried. Indeed, we should draw some consolation from the fact that the followers of Christ have always botched things significantly, letting this fact soften our own hearts toward humility. The recent shenanigans of the Vatican are nothing new. People have always had to fight for their integrity and freedom in the church, and some of our greatest saints have suffered from abusive church officials. Why the people who become powerholders in the church so often forget this is one of the many sub-puzzles of the mystery of iniquity. Why recent Vatican leaders have so thoroughly repressed the reasons for the success, the evangelical fruits, of the pontificate of John XXIII is more of the same. But those of us sure that God can be no sexist, no lover of power plays, no vetoer of intellectual freedom have to stand firm in the face of this absurdity. As Bernard Lonergan has said, sometimes what we most need is the inverse insight that there is nothing to understand. Sin is irrational. If an action does not make sense to people of sound mind and good heart, it is a sin.

After such an inverse insight, fidelity to God means continuing on, sadder but wiser. One has to keep battling to represent feminist convictions in one's teaching and writing, even if that brings official disapproval. One has to keep trying to reform the curricula infected by sexist disregard of women. With humor, with patience, without a martyr's complex, one has to rejoice in the struggles that just may be a tiny share in Christ's redemptive sufferings. Esther, one of our good role models, said, "If I perish, I perish." De Caussade, an interesting prober of the depths of Christian fidelity, spoke sensibly about abandonment to

33

divine providence. These may seem lofty references for so lowly a struggle as representing feminist perspectives in university or church circles frequently is, yet I find them consoling.

If we are theologians, workers in the area of religious studies who have and want to develop constructive explanations rooted in personal experience, we cannot let such matters of meeting our students' needs and rendering intellectual justice stand divorced from fidelity to God. We have to join our three obligations in something whole, something alive with the breath of the divine Spirit. Ultimately, all of our efforts and time exit into God's mystery. What we do in the classroom and in faculty meetings is as much part of our oblation as what we do in the chapel, in the bedroom, at the word processor. We have to love all the uses of our time even as we surrender them all to the God whom none of us has ever seen. We have to trust that all of them may be taken by the One to whom we look for salvation as tokens that we have made an effort. Even when our hearts condemn us for laziness, cowardness, impure motivation, and myriad other failings, we have to believe that God is greater than our hearts and knows everything. As we forgive God for being so good, and forgive the obtuse or malicious for being so difficult, we have to forgive ourselves for being imperfect, unlovely, unfaithful.

The justification for our inevitably mottled and less than fully successful efforts to integrate feminist perspectives into the religious studies curriculum finally comes from the foundations of such self-forgiveness, which are the foundations of our entire being and faith. They come not from ourselves but from God, the great maker of religious studies. We don't belong to ourselves, and our religious studies don't derive from ourselves. They derive from the mysterious Beginning and Beyond we call God, just as they point to God. What they have to say about women therefore is a matter of what God implies for women and men. If God implies that all human beings are precious images of a source uniquely able to set our hearts on fire, then women's right to appear in religious studies as the equals of men is well secured. If God implies that the salvation of both sexes from sin entails overcoming the alienations they have inflicted upon one another, then women's right to appear in religious studies as the equals of men is grounded in the bedrock of human need--the pain and hope that go below sexual differentiation to the crux of rational animality. In the final analysis, then, we should attempt to integrate feminist perspectives into our religious studies curricula because we want to keep faith with our God.

IV

MASCULINE AND FEMININE DIMENSIONS OF THE DIVINE

The task here is to relate Christian theology--
sense of God--to spirituality, sexuality, and intimacy.
It is a welcome task, because it puts in play matters
of great moment. For believers, nothing is more
interesting than theology. To ponder the divine
mystery that gives us our being and hope brings great
delight. Nor is such pondering merely abstract or
academic. The difference between the theology that
nourishes spirituality--the awakening of our minds and
hearts in love--and the theology that merely gives
academic credits is as wide as the Grand Canyon. One
thinks of Pascal, underscoring the difference between
the God of Abraham, Isaac, and Jacob and the God of the
philosophers. One thinks of Thomas a Kempis, insisting
that the point is to feel compunction, not know its
definition. Unless we connect with God, pray to God,
feel what it would be like to love the Lord, our God,
with whole mind, heart, soul, and strength, we are of
all believers the most to be pitied. God has made us
for himself, herself, and our hearts are restless until
they rest in God. So spirituality bears directly on
the Christian understanding of God and vice-versa.
Not those who say, "Lord, Lord," but those who do God's
will enter into the real treasures of faith. Not those
who give conference lectures but those who pray with
repentant hearts please the Christ who forged the
parable of the pharisee and the publican.

Our sexuality is also intriguing, weighty, fit
matter for theological reflection and our hunger to
know about God. The Bible speaks of men and women
knowing one another sexually, implying that some
wisdoms only come through touch and embrace. When the

prophets urge Israel to know the Lord, and lament Israel's ignorance of Torah, something sexual lingers. Ignorance of the Lord is part of an ugly infidelity. Not to walk in the way of Torah is to abandon the lover who has longed to treat his people like a bride. Jesus lamented the fact that so many of his countrymen and countrywomen did not know the things for their peace. Paul spoke of union with Christ as making believers one body with him. The intimacy of husband and wife, parent and child, friend and friend runs through page after page of the Bible, suggesting the closeness that God wants to have with us. God is more intimate to us than we are to ourselves. God would espouse us with cords of love, tying us to the covenant the way a good man ties a willing woman or a good woman ties a willing man.

These are some of the first thoughts, the warm-up exercises, that this topic has raised for me. Let us now develop them more formally in terms of three topics: masculine dimensions of God, feminine dimensions of God, and practical implications.

1. Masculine Dimensions of God

It is axiomatic for Christian theologians that God is beyond sex and gender. We can predicate of God anything decently drawn from human experience, but we always have to confess that what we say about God is more unlike than like the divine reality. So the analogies that we develop are only a thin thread, nothing we can lean upon without caution. Still, we are bound to use analogies, rooted as our spirituality is in our bodies and imaginations. And such use is sanctioned, even encouraged, by the Incarnation: if the Word of God took flesh, fleshly things can be wonderful revelations of God. Eastern Christianity answered the question about fleshly revelations of God once and for all during the iconoclast controversy. In deciding that icons are legitimate, even imperative, Eastern Christians went to the roots of the Incarnation and found all worship of "Christ our God" to be sacramental.

This said, it remains pertinent that the majority of the biblical images for God picture the divinity as masculine. Indeed, for Christians the masculinity of God is compounded, since the man Jesus of Nazareth is God's primal image. For present purposes, the salient aspects of these facts would seem to be less the speculative implications they might bear than their implications for our spirituality, our flesh and blood faith. What can we refine of the traditional imagery that depicts God as a King, a Lord, a Master, so that masculine experience provides us a window onto the divine lover we now only glimpse through a glass darkly but hope one day to see face to face?

One aspect of God that social conditioning is likely to make us consider masculine is God's being in charge. Throughout history, men have tended to be in charge--of the states, the armies, the churches, the schools, the businesses, the extended families. Sometimes this leadership and control has been benevolent. Often it has been self-serving, justifying the bad odor now attaching to the word "patriarchy." But almost always it has been a fundamental fact: men have had more official power than women, so the Power running the universe, working salvation, has been imagined to be masculine.

Let us admit that this legacy can cause problems nowadays yet postpone to another day the negative aspects of God's control, so that we can concentrate on the positive aspects. From the benevolent dimensions of power, guidance, responsibility, direction, and the like, we may refresh our appreciation of creation and providence. Take the man (or woman) who is competent. Recently I read a short story of John Updike in which a traveling salesman, discovering that the burning pain in his stomach that he had attributed to peanuts and drinks consumed on the plane would not go away, checked himself into a hospital of a strange city for what turned out to be an emergency appendectomy. The turning point in the story is the scene in which a senior surgeon finally solves the mystery of the man's pain, which is atypical of appendicitis, and competently effects the surgery. What a comfort finally to be understood and cured! What a relief to find order, meaning, and healing restored! The salesman is amused at his reduction to a childlike dependence, but that does not diminish the gratitude he feels. Without confidence that someone understands, that things are making sense, all of us feel fear and unease. We are made for understanding and being understood, for meaning and sense. Ultimately, only God can supply meaning and sense in cosmic measure. Ultimately, only God is responsible for the world, including the incredibly intricate world of our bodies. Certainly future reflection on God will do well to import large measures of the meaning, ordering, and comfort one instinctly associates with the Madonna, the mother-image burned into all of our psyches from earliest infancy. But past reflection also did well when it moved from a sense of responsibility especially associated with masculine maturity to speak about divine providence.

Because God made the world, and God's making continued moment by moment, keeping each creature in being, for faith nothing was absurd. Everything could have its meaning, even though frequently that meaning might escape limited, sinful human beings, who could never mount to a God's-eye view. For such venerable spiritual writers as Père de Caussade, who wrote the classical treatise on holy abandonment to divine providence, God's responsibility and trustworthiness meant that giving one's life over into God's care was the wisest thing one could do. Who would take better care of one's truly best interests than God? If given the choice between relying on one's own wisdom and entrusting one's life to God, would not only a fool choose self-reliance?

I realize, of course, that a proper self-reliance is an important part of any mature person's profile. One of the customary features of divine providence, in fact, seems to be to force us to take responsibility for the selves we become, by showing us that nothing human can substitute for God. This is the lesson read out to us in the biblical attacks on idolatry. It is what the Wisdom literature implies when it tells us not to put our trust in princes. But the final lesson of the biblical program for maturation is that we have to turn our self-sufficiency over to God, realizing that death merely dramatizes a limitation we have always suffered and that everything meritorious in us belongs to God's grace.

One might accept this reading of divine providence, this extrapolation from the benign effects of masculine competence and responsibility, and still wonder whether it isn't too good to be true. If so, some imagery of Jesus himself becomes most interesting. For not only did Jesus speak of God's care for the lilies of the field, saying that even followers of little faith had to be dearer to the Father than his flowers, Jesus also gave us the parable of the father running out to meet the prodigal son. In fact the lesson seems to be that God is the prodigal one, more generous, forgiving, simply good than we find it comfortable to imagine. For Jesus it was inconceivable that, asked for bread, the Father would give anyone a stone. It was inconceivable that those who asked in Jesus's name would not receive good measure, pressed down and overflowing.

So, perhaps there is something well worth saving in the images of control and authority traditionally associated with the masculine dimension of God. Perhaps our faith that providence is prevailing can continue to be well-mediated by speech reflecting Jesus's trust in his Father. The Lord whom Israel worshiped was compassionate and merciful, long-suffering and abounding in steadfast love, as well as a fearsome foe to the wicked. When Israel was a child, the Lord loved Israel. When Israel acted like Hosea's unfaithful wife Gomer, the Lord continued to love Israel. From this, no doubt, came Jesus's confidence that God is willing to forgive us seventy-times seven. The rule of the biblical God, his Kingdom, is as gentle and kindly as it is efficient. Though the nations rage and evolution wreaks great carnage, faith in the Father of Jesus says that God will supply both meaning and justice. Depending on the Father of Jesus, Christians have been able to find their lives full of wonders.

2. Feminine Dimensions of God

Feminist biblical scholars, such as Phyllis Trible, have scoured the imagery of God in Scripture and noted that although masculine figures prevail, feminine figures are also present. Most famous, perhaps, is Isaiah's figure of a nursing mother. If a nursing mother could not abandon her child, no matter what the child's outrageous behavior, certainly the Lord would never abandon Israel. Equally important is the figure of Jeremiah that has God moved to the divine womb by compassion for Israel. The love of God for Israel is like that inalienable bond that a mother has for the child she has conceived and carried for nine months. The child is flesh of her flesh, so nothing the child ever does or becomes removes it from the healthy mother's interest, compassion, and love.

One can also note the figure of the Spirit of God brooding over creation, the image of Jesus wanting to gather and shelter his people the way that a hen gathers and shelters her chicks, and the description of divine Wisdom as a gracious Lady. Inasmuch as Christian spirituality associated Wisdom with the Holy Spirit, it somewhat feminized the Holy Spirit. Then the Pauline figure of the Spirit making believers' prayer with sighs too deep for words called to mind birth-pangs, as even more clearly did the Pauline figure of all creation in labor for redemption.

It would be historically untrue and psychologically naive to think that these feminine images for God counterbalanced the influence of patriarchy in either Jewish or Christian spirituality. Yet it would be equally untrue and naive not to realize that such patriarchy never has been the final word. For saints such as Julian of Norwich, Hildegard of Bingen, and Teresa of Avila, Christian spirituality had to be something that fulfilled their given personhood, which was thoroughly feminine. Thus Julian thought of Christ as mothering his followers and nourishing them at the breast. Hildegard, like her fellow medieval mystic Mechtild of Magdeburg, thought of creation as God's original blessing, more full of grace than marred by sin, and she stressed the goodness of the human body in ways anticipating recent efforts of holistic spiritual writers. Teresa of Avila is famous for the nuptial symbolism in which she expressed her mystical experiences of God, as well as for her hard-headed practicality about the reform of Carmelite convents. In their different ways, all of these outstanding women found the Christian tradition large enough to accommodate their feminine needs. Patriarchy never meant that God wasn't enough like them to understand their needs and longings. Faith always meant that God retained the priority, and so that whatever they found to be noble, true, and good in their feminine worlds reflected favorably on God.

Present-day spiritual writers such as Monika Hellwig have continued to bring distinctively feminine insights to bear on their study of God. For example, Hellwig has written of Christ as the compassion of God, moving Christology far away from the legalistic categories in which much traditional discussion of redemption traded. Other feminist scholars have worked at rehabilitating the significance of the Virgin Mary, showing the large measure of femininity that the Virgin brought into popular Christian piety during the patristic and medieval eras. For Protestant Christianity, the prominence of women in the churches of the left wing of the Reformation, where charismatic gifts flourished, suggested the compatibility between feminine spirituality and the God moving people to fresh encounters with the vivifying Spirit. For Eastern Christianity, the veneration accorded the Mother of God, the Theotokos, assured that religion would retain a kindly, maternal dimension.

These brief references to the history of Christian spirituality do not cover over the fact that theology proper paid more attention to the stereotypically masculine attributes of God than to stereotypically feminine attributes. But they do suggest that people usually had no doubt that all goodness and love, whatever its sexual overtones, came from God and reflected the divine goodness. When the Johannine literature made love the best human analogy to God, it opened the way to Christians' considering the warmth of women a sign of the divine affection for human beings.

Today's raised consciousness about women's issues suggests that we develop the seeds of a feminist understanding of God into a full appreciation of how closely many women's instincts resemble the apparent intentions of God. Thus women's stereotypical concern for concrete people rather than abstract principles can seem a reflection of the Jesus who pronounced the Sabbath made for human beings rather than human beings for the Sabbath. It can also seem to reflect the God who wants mercy rather than sacrifice and who expects us to forgive others as She has forgiven us. Similarly, women's tendency to think holistically, linking mind and body, and their instinct to view ecological conservation as more significant than companies' needs to increase their profits, can seem providential reminders of the values that the biblical God probably is trying to promote nowadays. This is not to say, of course, that many men do not agree with such instincts, but it is to point out that women's traditional aversion to legalism and violence now squares with what both a fully adequate spirituality and the survival of the earth seem to require of us.

Because of their involvement with birth and nurture, women have been socialized to protect the vulnerable and hate the impersonal forces responsible for so much pain throughout history. It strikes women as madness to keep building weapons of awesome destructive potential, to keep developing chemicals that poison the earth from which we draw our food, the water we drink, the air we breathe. Such madness contradicts the uterine love mentioned by the prophet Jeremiah. It puts an ache in the center of us women, because it threatens a major biological role we have played. Whether or not a given woman has borne children, she has been socialized since infancy to think of herself as a carrier and nurse of life. From this background present-day women might well draw some highly relevant images of the divine maternity that would ease their prayer and strengthen their resolve to fight for peace and the earth's preservation.

God is the ultimate source of all being and life in the universe. This conviction stands forth in the first verses of the Bible and the first articles of the Christian creed. But how could God be such a source without possessing the sort of fertility associated with women? Most of the religions outside the pale of the Bible sensed the kinship of women's fertility with the source of being and life. No doubt the biblical theologians were right in fearing the intrusion of sexuality into their conception of God, but their fear tended to blind them to more positive possibilities. For example, the veneration that the Canaanites showed fertility could be a source of profound thanksgiving for the divine creativity, as well as a potential source of orgiastic excesses.

Similarly, the veneration that Buddhists have shown the feminine Wisdom that has gone beyond this-worldly ignorance and the cosmic womb from which all beings derive now strikes many theologians as offering positive theological possibilities. Because we so desperately need a religious symbolism that will help us to protect life, guard the earth, and move our economics and politics toward greater justice for the wretched of the world, we ought to be especially grateful for images that remind us of God's stake in creation. From the divine substance God has drawn forth a world of great intricacy, extent, power, and fragility. As the species let in on God's secrets, enabled by our reason to appreciate the sweep of God's work, we human beings have both the privilege and the responsibility of protecting that to which God has given birth. Whatever exists solicits from us respect and a proper reverence. We should hurt nothing casually, carelessly, inadvertently. Many aboriginal peoples realized this far better than Christians have. Asking the forgiveness of the animal or plant they had to take for food, such peoples expressed their deep appreciation of the gratuity of creation. Because they had not made the world, had not created the animals and plants, they had no right to abuse them. On occasion they did in fact abuse them, but apparently with far more realization of the sacrilege involved than we moderns have shown.

In a word, then, the feminine dimensions of divinity spotlight the divine concern to bring forth life and help it prosper. God is always on the side of justice and love, always against injustice and heartlessness. If we find this hard to verify in the record of evolution, we might more fully commit ourselves to the teachings of Christ. There it is plain that God only moves in our world from motives of love. The forces of nature subserve a divine sense of purpose and harmony that escape our ken, as the Lord made clear to Job, while the forces of sin that human beings have unleashed in the world show the extent of God's desire to keep people free to say yes or no to the divine overtures of love.

Our being able to sin is the price of our being able to accept God's love and respond with whole mind, heart, soul, and strength. Why we human beings find it so difficult to accept God's love and respond, why we are so prone to sin and destroy ourselves, remains the great puzzle of human existence. To my mind, Christ crucified and resurrected sheds the most significant light on it, and that light mainly calls for our further magnifying the goodness of God. Even though we often close our hearts to God, God is greater than our hearts and has assured us that where sin has abounded grace has abounded the more. Pondering this greater abounding of grace, we may increasingly feel that we are not motherless children, adrift in an uncaring universe, but are the apple of our Creator's eye.

3. Practical Implications

In reflecting on the utility of a stereotypically masculine attribute of God, such as the divine control of the world, and a stereotypically feminine attribute, such as the divine concern for the welfare of God's children, we have anticipated some of the practical implications God's transcendence of human limitations can carry. Whatever helps men and women appreciate the goodness of God and the depths of revelation should be admitted into their prayer and social action.

Suppose, for instance, that a woman who found it hard to believe in God's care benefitted from thinking of God as like her kindhearted mother or like her fully trustworthy sister. Would she not be entirely justified in deepening this conception of God, furthering her exploration of the divine femininity? Both common sense and traditional spiritual counsel suggest that she would. God is fully parental and fully friendly. We can find reflections of God in every decent form of love, fidelity, and helpfulness. One implication of the spotlight thrown on the riches of divinity by our current concern with gender is that the limits of our appreciation of God's affinity to our sexual characteristics are only the limits of our imagination. Certainly God always goes beyond our images, but images that make creation more intelligible and redemption more credible are precious beyond price.

The same lessons hold for men seeking to explore the divine beauty by contemplating the femininity of God, women seeking to explore the divine strength by contemplating the masculinity of God, either sex seeking to appreciate better the divine goodness by thinking of God as better than the best of human parents. If we experience erotic love as a wonderful source of energy and hope, we should apply erotic love to its ultimate font, the God who has been romancing creation since time out of mind. If we experience self-sacrifice as a marvel that stops our tongues and forces us to wonder about Christ's cross, we should realize that all self-sacrifice, that of women and that of men, can become an icon of God's unfathomable love.

God so loved the world he gave us the best that he had to give, his only begotten son. If it would increase our appreciation of this gift, we should change the language of the traditional translation so that it read, "the best that she had to give, her only begotten son." Perhaps then the Latin American mothers weeping over their children who have "disappeared," the mothers grieving years after for children sacrificed to war, and even the mothers heartsick at the turmoil introduced into their children's lives by drugs would stand in bolder relief. God suffers with us, in us, we believe, wanting our flourishing even more than we do. As Saint Irenaeus put it, the glory of God is human beings fully alive. Whatever gender imagery helps us to let such traditional truths feed our faith is not only desirable but imperative.

Another practical implication of expanding our appreciation of the bisexuality, and the transsexuality, of God is to free up our sense of human equality. The traditional notion that human beings are images of God, reflections of the divine creativity, reason, and love, has to apply equally to women and men, lest Eve and Adam stand for two different shares in God's bounty. At many periods of Christian history, leading theologians considered women deficient human beings. Men were the primary instances of humanity, and so the primary images of God, and women were secondary instances, derivative and lesser. But the priestly account of creation in Genesis makes it plain that from the beginning the humanity that was to be an image of the Creator was male and female. Each sex reflected its divine source, and only the coordination of the sexes yielded either a full humanity or a full imagining of God.

It is another task, for another day, to explain why women have had to struggle to be accounted fully human, but on this occasion it seems clear that exploring the femininity of God should only increase our ability to see women as full images of God. Others can speculate about the political, economic, and cultural consequences that such theology ought to inspire. It strikes me that a church such as my Roman Catholic, which still worries about considering women the full equals of men, at least when it comes to sharing church power, probably will find contemplations of the divine sexuality unsettling. It also strikes me that such an unsettling could be salutary. If God has a feminine dimension to match the masculine dimension that took flesh in Christ, in Christ there need be neither male nor female, as Paul put it, because in Christ all human beings can achieve their deepest reflection of God.

A third practical implication of expanding our appreciation of the divine masculinity and femininity concerns intimacy between men and women. If they find their sexuality grounded in God, will women and men be better able to deal with one another as friends, rather than as intimate enemies? I suspect and hope that they will. The differences between women and men certainly will continue, because biology and social conditioning will continue to function. But if our spirituality, our existential religion, were to make us more comfortable with the femininity of God, then the interactions between men and women of faith could be warmer and more trusting. Each sex could think that in following its attraction to the other it was pursuing a species of the divine beauty and goodness. Men, especially, might feel healed of the division that their desire for women sometimes creates, realizing that being drawn to women's beauty is a movement one may attribute to the Holy Spirit. Instead of fearing sexual attraction, both sexes might deepen it and make it saner. When we place sexual attraction among the works of the Holy Spirit, we are less likely to lose perspective about it and more likely to become amused and gracious.

For the fact is that sexual differentiation is a funny, as well as a brilliant, way to structure reproduction and raise hope for a divine lover who would bring us complete fulfillment. God might have had us reproduce like the amoeba, simply splitting and filling out. But apparently God wanted human life to begin in the most moving of human experiences, fully-felt sexual attraction and love. This is the reason, Scripture says, that young men and women leave home and cleave to one another. This is the force reflecting the divine fecundity and courage. The act of faith that God made in bringing the world into being and creating a species capable of loving God back continues in the acts of faith that God's images make each time they say yes to love and commit themselves to making life go on.

From the primal experience of sexual love human beings grow to parental love, the love of educators, the love of citizens, and all the other ways that we care for the earth that God has given us. By the end of our lives, psychologists such as Erik Erikson tell us, we should have made peace with this whole process, realizing that, whatever our defects, it was necessary that we suffer and love just as we have, because somehow we were serving a higher plan. When we love, we feel and act more widely, with fuller implications, than we can imagine, just as when we refuse to love we further longstanding patterns of sin.

In the final analysis, our lives repose with Christ in the mystery of God, and of course our sexuality goes with us. The mystery of God, we may be sure, has better purposes for our femininity and masculinity than we have ever fathomed. Ultimately, one of God's best purposes must be our expressing the limitless divine beauty and goodness. Precisely as men and women, we bear forth into the world reflections of God's own competence and tenderness, God's own masculinity and femininity. Shuffled around, freed of their stereotypical limitations, the competence of God becomes a support of our femininity, while the tenderness of God becomes a support of our masculinity. If all this implies that the most practical thing we can do with the sexuality of God is to play with it freely and faithfully, I hope we will all be both amused and encouraged.

V

WOMEN IN THE CHURCH

1. Personal Experience in the Church

I grew up in Baltimore (Highlandtown) as a cradle Catholic, went to St. Bridgid's Church, attended the Institute of Notre Dame, and joined the School Sisters of Notre Dame. Throughout this youth, the church and faith were as much atmospheric as things I explicitly focused upon--I took them for granted like the air I breathed. This was so mainly because of my mother, a woman with little formal education but much intelligence and even more faith. It was natural for her to discuss her problems with the Blessed Mother, and as a little girl, the youngest of her five children, I sometimes overheard her. All the more so did faith become her mainstay when she lost my father when I was seven and my second oldest brother in World War II shortly thereafter. My mother managed the four boys and me through hard work and taking one day at a time, as God disposed it to her. When two of my brothers went into religious life, and I then followed, she could not have been prouder.

My sixteen years in religious life were instructive and deeply satisfying. They bridged the old, pre-Vatican II church and the new, post-Vatican II church, and they gave me considerable experience of teaching, confirming my sense that teaching was my religious vocation. The graduate studies I did in philosophy at Boston College provided the opportunity to learn a more adequate language in which to articulate the experiences central to Christian living, and when I left religious life to marry it was with little sense of discontinuity, though with considerable sorrow about the pains that institutional Catholicism seemed determined to inflict on those who challenged it.

It was somewhat ironic, therefore, that my first job was teaching philosophy at a seminary in California run by the same Sulpicians whom my uncle had served in Baltimore as their provincial. In California I saw at first hand the few good effects, and the many bad, of sending young boys to isolated seminary high schools and colleges, and consistently I was both amused and irritated at the treatment accorded us few women faculty members. The nadir of such treatment came when the president of the college called me in to tell me he might have to fire me. It was nothing personal, he hastened to assure me. In fact he hoped that I would chair the philosophy department the coming year. But Archbishop McGucken had learned that there was an ex-nun teaching at the seminary (though he did not know my name), and he told the college president to find some pretext--any pretext--for firing her. To his credit, the president was by now red-faced, and he insisted that he had told the Archbishop that firing me was the last thing he wanted to do. But he felt he had to warn me of the possibility that I would become a bee in the Archbishop's bonnet. I remember driving home on the freeway and pondering the image that had welled up from my depths to express how I felt. A great steamroller was lumbering along an asphalt street, relentlessly advancing toward a little bug.

In the event, the bug survived, continued to work both at the seminary and as the religious education director of a prosperous parish, and for the first years of her marriage drew from this church work most of the money she and her husband lived on, Stanford graduate stipends needing much supplement. The marriage ceremony itself was one of those privileged times when a community of friends finds its love perfectly expressed and founded sacramentally. The home liturgy group my husband John had led turned the marriage into a great celebration, and my cousin Jerry, a Sulpician teaching at my seminary, represented both my family and the school.

Once again, however, the ironic, pathetic aspects of our situation and church reality had their say. With the permission from Rome to marry had come, in a Latin under which some Cardinal had scrawled his name illegibly, certain further provisions we had not anticipated. First, there was an ipso facto legitimation of the bastards it was assumed or feared we had generated. Second, there was a command to move 500 miles away and not have our marriage entered on the parish register, lest we give scandal. Third, there was a command not to teach religion or theology. All of this brought us to one of those clear moments of decision, one of those crossroads that memory never gives up: were we to laugh or to cry, to howl in amusement or in fury? We chose to laugh and, fortified by both good friends and a stiff drink, to count our little encounter with Rome a rite of passage. In a way beyond our calculating or control, we were radicalized: forced to look at the roots of what had been our natal religious community, our longstanding spiritual home, and see what on earth or in heaven could justify our remaining in it.

As the Decree on Ecumenism (paragraph 11) published by Vatican II expressed it, there is a "hierarchy of truths" in Christian faith. That hierarchy was very important to us, because it helped separate the wheat of the Trinity, Grace, and the Incarnation (Karl Rahner's three "cardinal" Christian truths) from the chaff of lesser aspects and traditions, including the forms in which the Vatican had grown accustomed to expressing the Petrine ministry. The recent contretemps between such Vatican officials as Cardinal Ratzinger and progressive theologians the world over has brought "the hierarchy of truths" back to the center of theological discussion. The Cardinal would like to dilute the significance of Vatican II's teaching on this point and make every pronouncement of the magisterium something that the faithful, theologians and laity alike, are to accept with no dissent, no matter how protestedly loyal. I have so long loved that little gift from the Decree on Ecumenism, that formal teaching that there is a center and a periphery, that of course I'm not going to give it up. It will return at the end of this chapter, when I discuss a loyal feminist opposition to the lack of faith and charity that the Vatican has been manifesting too frequently recently.

Quickly to finish what is relevant from the rest of my biography, I need only say that after our tour in California we went to Penn State University, finding there such mental disease in the Religion Department that we again willy-nilly were radicalized, this time with regard to academic institutions. Penn State also had little vibrant church life, so it was a relief to find better fare for both our professional and personal lives in Wichita, Kansas, where next we gave it a try. In Wichita John began to write full-time and I progressed through the ranks to full professor and chair of the religion department. We made good friends, founded a little home church, and were surprised to find that a lot of companies wanted to publish us. I furthered work I had begun on women and religion at Penn State (where the topic had been considered a useless fad), and published a book under the title of <u>Women and World Religions</u> for use in college courses. By the time that we had left Wichita State, to accept a generous offer from the University of Tulsa, we had published about twenty-five books, some of them dealing expressly with Catholic theology.

As chair of the faculty of religion at the University of Tulsa I have had the opportunity to bring religious studies into the mainstream of the Tulsa Curriculum, a general education sequence that has gotten some national notice for its reassertion of a quite traditional emphasis on the arts and sciences. I also have been directing the Warren Center for Catholic Studies, which brings to campus distinguished visiting professors and lecturers. Neither Wichita nor Tulsa qualifies as a progressive Catholic diocese (the bishop of Wichita warned us not to come, and the bishop of Tulsa is one of the seven or so who did not approve the pastoral letter on the US economy), but in both places we have found people keeping the grassroots green. Our faith has not taken the path one might think ideal, because the given parish structures have offered so little nourishment, yet we have continued to mine the riches of the Catholic tradition, and to try to laugh more than weep. This resolution was tested last Christmas, when we made a rare visit to the cathedral. There the sermon for ten o'clock Mass on Christmas Day dealt in gruesome detail with the "rivers of blood" caused by the horrible sin of abortion. I find abortion chilling and tragic, but it isn't the first thing that comes to mind when I gather with others to celebrate the enfleshment of God's word, the arrival of the blessed child of light and love. Whether I am right or wrong, the fact continues to be that I seem to be out of phase with many who represent church power nowadays, and this makes me muse quite frequently about why our times seem to be so painfully out of joint.

2. Scenes of Women from Biblical and Church History

We go to scripture and tradition for many legitimate reasons, but certainly one such reason is to be consoled and challenged by stories of how others coped with their times, which of course also frequently appeared to be out of joint. Consider, for example, Ruth, who stands as a paradigm of biblical faith, because the loss of her husband only increased her devotion to her mother-in-law Naomi and eventually led to her marriage to Boaz and the furtherance of the bloodline that produced both David and Jesus. The bond between Ruth and Naomi caused me to reflect in a recent work as follows: "The short story turns out well, of course, and at the happy ending we are allowed to think that God has rewarded the women's fidelity. But long before the fruition of their hopes in the child who would become the grandfather of King David, the women have started to enjoy success in their venture. By bonding together, weeping and laughing together, they immediately begin to cut their fears down to size. By trekking back to Bethlehem side by side, they greatly diminish the hardships of the journey. Simply by being together, by opening their hearts in mutual love, they have gained a pearl of great price. The happy aftermath is but a fitting setting from which their love can the better shine" (<u>Biblical Woman</u> [New York: Crossroad, 1988], pp. 34-35). In other words, when the times are out of joint, our ties to those who share our faith may become the stronger, and so the central biblical theme of God's bringing light out of darkness may reach out to embrace us.

The love of Christ reached out to embrace such women of the New Testament era as the Samaritan discussed in John 4. Fresh from her encounter with Jesus by the well, she rushed off to tell her friends, "He told me all that I ever did" (John 4:39). It is meeting with God that brings any of us the deepest self-knowledge. It has been meeting God, finding their portion of the lovely Wisdom of God, that has kept countless Christian women going. Consider Monica, the mother of Saint Augustine, whose tears and fussing finally gained the reward of seeing her son baptized. Consider the medieval visionaries Hildegard and Mechtild, whose perception of the goodness of creation, of the original blessing that breathes deep down in all that God has made, has inspired a corps of present-day Christian ecologists, including the controversial Dominican Matthew Fox. Then there is Teresa of Avila, buffeted by the churchpeople opposed to her reforms of the Carmelites, yet carried by her meetings with Christ to utter the remarkable words of advice, "Let nothing disturb you." And the tradition continues today with such arresting women as Rosemary Haughton, the brilliant spiritual writer, mother of ten, and defender of the homeless in Gloucester, Massachusetts. Haughton's own study of New Testament women, The Re-Creation of Eve (Springfield, IL: Templegate, 1985) brings them alive in all their angular, idiosyncratic humanity, reminding us that Mary the Mother of Jesus, Mary Magdalene, the sisters of Lazarus, and the rest were all women of flesh and blood, struggling to comprehend the whirlwind that Jesus had set in their hearts, doing their best to remain faithful, as their standing by the cross shows they did.

One of the best fruits of the rise of feminist scholarship in religion has been the production of numerous historical studies that document how women have always fought through to a viable spirituality, in all the traditions, East and West. In the Christian case, the work of Elisabeth Schussler Fiorenza on the status of women in the New Testament, of Elizabeth Clark on the status of women during the patristic era, of Rosemary Ruether and her several collaborators who have gathered studies of women in medieval, reformation, and American Christian history, and many other feminist scholars, has been making it plain that though Christian women virtually never have been accepted by official Christianity as the equals of men, virtually always they have provided the church much more than half of its heart and soul. One thinks of Catherine of Siena, badgering the pope to quit Avignon, go back to Rome, and start reforming the church lest the moral stench of the clergy make faith entirely impossible. One thinks of Clare, companion of Francis, and all the freedom and joy that Franciscan poverty has given the church. Mother Teresa of Calcutta, Nobel Laureate for Peace, continues this tradition today. Whatever one thinks of her traditional views of the roles of women, one has to be grateful for her brilliant demonstration that love of the poorest is a sure hallmark of the divine presence.

The saints I have mentioned are women who found

their way to the center of the Christian mystery and so were able to keep peripheral matters in proper perspective. Compared to the divine life that membership in the Body of Christ had brought into their souls, even the sins of the popes were secondary. We know less about the women whose church membership came close to breaking them, but as we trust that the Spirit of God supported their deepest prayers, too, crying out with sighs too deep for words, we are wise to let their sufferings sober us. Phyllis Trible's book, <u>Texts of Terror</u> (Philadelphia: Fortress, 1984), deals with such Old Testament women as Hagar, the concubine raped and left for dead, and the daughter of Jephthah, sacrificed to death by his stupid vow. In each case we find women abused and maimed in function of Israelite business as usual. No compassion inculcated by faith in the Israelite Lord flowed out to protect them. In their cases the steamroller kept rolling, so they had to commend their spirits to the darkness, hoping against hope that on the other side of their crushing fate God would provide for them.

I would extend such pathos to the apparently lesser cases of injustice, with which history is rife, in which women of great potential found themselves frustrated by the social and ecclesiastical ground rules of their day. I would extend such pathos to the many Roman Catholic women who today feel themselves called to ordination and meet only an ecclesiastical stone wall. Even the women torn and twisted by decisions about contraception and divorce have frequently suffered from an apparently inhumane, legalistic church. Not having admitted women's voice into its canon law or traditional moral theology, the Catholic church should not be amazed to find many women feeling alienated, misunderstood, without standing or significance.

The history of women is only beginning to emerge from the underside of our past. The concerns of the majority of women throughout history--family life, children, a network of friends, the chance to feel the mercy and love of God--have been of little interest to mainstream historians, as they have been of little interest to mainstream theologians. Rosemary Haughton makes much of the feminine Wisdom that, from biblical times to the present, has represented another reading of history. In that reading, nothing is more important than the bread broken and joy shared around family tables, than the quiet determination that the children would get a chance at a better life and that the brutality of war and politics would stop at the hall closet, where the men took off their soiled coats and muddied boots. Wisdom associated with the Virgin Mary, the Sorrowful Mother, sponsored a different religion from that of the movers and shakers. As Mary's "Magnificat" suggested, it was the little people, the population of the Beatitudes, upon whom God looked with warmest concern, and it was those proud in their hearts whom God had to scatter.

So the history of women's experience with Christianity has been more than the expectable blend of grace and sin. Because women so regularly were on the margins of official power, women tended to see more clearly than those holding office how much closer, more affective, and freer God's love frequently was than what the going laws or doctrines of the Church proposed. With a certain typical, perhaps even stereotypical directness, Christian women often went to God with confidence that even though the official church or the mainstream civil society had little place for them or their notions, God understood them completely and seconded much of the hope, desire, and love in their hearts.

3. Recent Developments Among Christian Feminists

I have noted that feminist scholarship has been retrieving the stories of women from the obscurity of historical neglect. Related to this retrieval has been a flowering of women's positive contributions to ethics, theology, and spirituality. Rosemary Ruether, for example, has written theological, as well as historical studies, aiming at extending the thesis that women are as fully human as men to the reform of our language about God and the development of ethical positions that protect the earth, target social justice, and champion the world's poor out of a sense of what one can only call maternal compassion. Phyllis Trible has studied the rhetoric of sexuality in the Bible, bringing out the minor key in which prophets such as Isaiah and Jeremiah sang of God's mothering love. If a nursing mother could never abandon her child, how much less could the God of Israel abandon her people. Monika Hellwig, working in the areas of sacramental theology and Christology, has correlated spirituality with a Christ whose first name is

compassion. Indeed, in her Madeleva Lecture on women's
spirituality (<u>Christian Women in a Troubled World</u> [New
York: Paulist, 1986]), Hellwig did not hesitate to
point out the advantages women's marginalization has
held, inasmuch as it has made women less prone to be
taken in by the legalism, or the commitment to models
stressing the desirability of power, that so regularly
have twisted both secular and ecclesiastical politics.

From the third world we are now starting to hear
the voices of women pointing out how machismo and
sexism are problems even for the very poor, who would
seem so abject that one might overlook such further
sources of pain. As well, feminist voices from the
third world, and from economic analysts in our own
nation, have underscored the fact that women and
children constitute the bulk of the very poor. Black
feminists, alert to both black machismo and epic
stereotypes of black women as saintly supermoms, have
begun to venture into the freighted question of racial
tensions and unfinished agendas between black and white
women. Since race and class, as well as gender, have
been modalities of oppression, to speak fully
adequately about a theology that would liberate women,
and men, one must become sensitive to many different
factors.

Fortunately, the techniques of consciousness
raising, networking, and conceiving of theology as a
collaborative enterprise that many Christian women have
found congenial are now starting to pay a rich
dividend. When one inquires about the sensibility, the
sort of awareness, that theology and spirituality
apparently will require if they are to serve us well in
the twenty-first century, many feminist traits leap to
mind. So many women have been in the forefront of
environmentalism, gun control, action against drunk
drivers, sex education, geriatrics, care of children,
the reform of work, and the dozens of other places in
our culture, national or global, that cry out for
redemption and a new start that it is inconceivable
that the church of the twenty-first century will not be
deeply committed to "women's issues," objectionable as
the phrase may be.

Let me concretize this point by referring to two
women I know who are both admirable church members and
may illustrate trends I find quite encouraging. Sydney
Thompson Brown is an active laywoman in the

Presbyterian church, and for decades she has been a deep ecumenist. With her husband Robert McAfee Brown, a leading Protestant ecumenist and liberation theologian, she has traveled to Cuba, Australia, and many other parts of the globe, broadening an internationalism formed by growing up in China. For the past twenty years or so, however, Sydney's special interest and expertise has been work: how to humanize it, how to integrate into the corporate world mothers and women with large family responsibilities, how to combat unemployment, how to make society at large realize the losses that come when managements limit their sense of responsibility and opportunity to the financial bottom line. She established a new-style employment agency in Palo Alto, then taught at Union Theological Seminary in New York, and recently has been working in Oakland. The more she has learned, gained experience, been applauded or rebuffed, the more the complexity of the issues, the intertwining of economics, politics, social prejudices, and judgments of faith, has come home to her. When I look for models of activist Christians bringing feminine experience and insight to bear on significant social issues, Sydney always comes to mind. She would rather do something-- organize a group, try to muster financial and emotional support, try to educate the local churches about their stake in the exodus of businesses or the employment of abused illegals--than debate the academic issues. Her sense of the church is more political than contemplative, more persuaded by evangelical scenes like Matthew 25, where Jesus separates the sheep from the goats on the basis of what they have done or failed to do, than by calls to prayer in secret. She would not deny the place of contemplation and secret prayer, but her large heart is most warmed by evidence that people with pain are receiving care, people who are hungry are receiving food, women who have felt themselves to be worthless, of no account, are being taken seriously and helped to flower.

Anne Patrick, who recently was our Warren Distinguished Visiting Professor at the University of Tulsa, is a traditional academic. Her regular appointment is at Carleton College, where she chairs the Religion Department, and her field is the border of ethics and literature. I watched her organize the program for the 1989 Annual Meeting of the Catholic Theological Society of America, of which she was the President-Elect. By both instinct and design, she sought out voices underrepresented in the past, and I have come to consider such an instinct characteristically feminist. The general theme of the 1989 convention was providence, so Anne enlisted a Sister of Providence interested in the theology of God's guidance of the world to give a major address. She worked hard to find Hispanic and Native American theologians, asking them to represent their traditions. Again and again, I noticed her effort to find a place on the program for teachers from smaller colleges, who often don't get a chance to give papers or moderate panels. In many cases whether or not their name appears on the program means the difference between receiving or not receiving financial support to attend the convention. So Anne seemed to me like a worried mother, trying to make sure that no straggler got lost.

Certainly many men are interested in the problem of work and deal with it compassionately. Certainly many men have put together conventions with great sensitivity to the responsibility of representing ideas or groups previously underrepresented. Yet when they have worked in this way, such men have been verifying the values of the biblical Wisdom that Haughton associates with both feminine sensitivities and the evangelical Christ. Men sure enough of their own identities not to be threatened by women's call for more reliance on love and freedom than on authority and law are serving such biblical Wisdom, as male Buddhist saints have always served the Prajnaparamita, the feminine personification of the Wisdom that has gone beyond this-worldly entanglements and offers the chance to see things as they really are.

If we have gotten as far afield as Mahayana Buddhism it must be time to bring this chapter to a close and summarize what ruminating on the topic of women in the church has led me to think is the heart of the matter. Two convictions stand out. The first is that all of the concern for health, the instinct for wholeness, and the insistence that love be kept at center stage and personalist values prevail--all of the aspects of a characteristically feminine Christian faith that we have been observing--mount what is to my mind an irresistible argument in favor of the hierarchy of truths taught by the Decree on Ecumenism and against the efforts of some curial officials to silence women, theologians, and any others so bold as to raise questions or show opposition to the unChristian conduct

61

of church business. Even if we were to keep silent, the very stones would cry out, because the living God is always on the side of intelligence, freedom, and love. The pharisaism that would stifle conscience and make people distrust their God-given experience is the enemy of the living God. That remains true even when we take to heart the position of many New Testament scholars that the historical Pharisees have not gotten a fair shake in the gospels. The mind-set that prefers rules to the liberty of the children of God is antipodal to the Spirit of Christ. The sabbath was made for human beings, not human beings for the sabbath. People should be ordained in the Christian community because they have the gifts for effective service, not because they are male. One can only think this way about church business, however, if one has a clear understanding of what is central to Christian faith and what is peripheral. Central is the divine life of love incarnate in Christ and his members. Central is the perception that everything is grace. Useful, good, but distinctly secondary are the Petrine ministry, the ministry of curial officials, and the particular, historically conditioned disciplinary rules or customs that the church has developed through the centuries.

Second, for those whose appreciation of women's history and present work in the church has galvanized them to a reading of Christian faith along these lines, loyal opposition to the pharisaism the church has shown in the past and continues to show today is natural, inevitable, and necessary. Usually it is not even especially painful, because one has already glimpsed, in some small measure, that the Christ was bound to suffer on the way to his glory, as the gospel of Luke puts it, and so that the members of Christ are likely to suffer as well. I hasten to add, of course, that nothing in the history or present experience of women in the church justifies a martyr's complex or a prideful, gnostic sense that we are pure and others are blind fools. No, all of us have sinned and fallen short of God's glory, as Paul puts it. But women can only stand by the truths that the Spirit has given them through the history of their experience in the church. We can only protest--speak forth our faith--as we actually believe. God help us, we Christian women have to trust that this will be enough.

VI

THE STORY OF WORLD RELIGIONS

A February 10, 1989 editorial in the New York
Times warned the Bush administration that in
reconsidering relations with Iran it would be foolish
to forget the cruelty associated with the regime of the
Ayatollah Khomeini. The central item in the
editorial's argument was the following: "In January,
according to the Iranian news agency, Ayatollah
Khomeini was deeply offended by a radio interview in
which a woman said she could not accept the prophet
Mohammed's daughter as a role model. As a result, the
broadcast director at the Teheran radio, Mohammad Arab
Mazar-Yazdi, was sentenced to five years in jail.
Three directors of the Teheran radio's Islamic ideology
group were sentenced to four years each. All received
50 lashes. The court levying these penalties held that
the broadcast 'notoriously misportrayed the ruling
mentality of Iranian women.' Had the insult been
deliberate, said the Ayatollah, the person responsible
would have been executed."

Stories such as these make the life of the teacher
of world religions both complicated and interesting.
On the one hand, students want to know how such things
could happen, how in the world sane people could
condemn others to flogging, imprisonment, or even death
because of a remark, probably quite innocent and
honest, that a traditional role model might no longer
be adequate. If one can fill in the background, and
explain some aspects of the authoritarian personality
that frequently shows up in the world religions, the
course in world religions can come alive. On the other
hand, it is distressing to confront the pathologies of

human existence, and perhaps most distressing to witness the corruption of what arguably is the deepest and best of the human passions, our hunger to know, love, and imitate the divine source of ourselves and our world. Let us turn over both sides of this situation, reflecting (1) on the historical context that any ethical action always presupposes and then dealing (2) with the tragedy one finds in the stories of the world religions. That should leave us poised (3) to discuss some of the implications the world religions carry for our own personal struggles to gain health and sanity.

1. Story and History

The Ayatollah Khomeini did not spring from the brow of Allah or Muhammad, like Athena from the brow of Zeus. He was formed by a long tradition of Shiite Islam. Among the most relevant aspects of that Shiite tradition stand the conflict between the Shiites and the Sunnis about the status of Muhammad's family, and the sufferings that Shiites have come to associate with religious fidelity.

The conflict between the Shiites and the Sunnis arose at the death of the Prophet Muhammad in 632. In choosing Muhammad's close disciple Abu Bakr as the Prophet's successor, the inner circle of early Islam opted for one of two theories of tribal succession then operative in Arabia. The stronger tradition probably was that a sheik or chieftain ought to be succeeded by the most competent of the men he had left behind. (Women were not eligible for such a position.) A second tradition held that blood relatives, especially eldest sons, ought to get special consideration. Muhammad had no sons. His closest male relative was his cousin and son-in-law Ali. The selection of Abu Bakr established the principle that blood ties were not going to be decisive in Muslim succession. Indeed, between the Prophet's death in 632 and the succession of Ali as the fourth caliph (ruler) in 656 stood 24 years and three intermediaries who were not blood relatives. Nonetheless, the partisans of Ali felt that from the beginning family members of the Prophet ought to have headed the Muslim community. The Shiites are the descendants of the party partisan to Ali. The Sunnis are the descendants of those who felt that Abu Bakr, and other caliphs who were not blood relatives, were legitimate successors.

However, the story is not so antiseptic and unemotional as we have made it thus far, because when Ali did finally come to power bad feeling overflowed. The strongest families of Mecca (what we might call the Arab aristocracy) opposed Ali, as did Muhammad's widow, Aisha, who was the daughter of Abu Bakr. Added to these tangles was the unfortunate fact that the third caliph, Ali's immediate predecessor, had been assassinated, and that Ali had neither protected him nor moved as caliph to punish his assassins. The next turn of this tragic screw was Ali's own assassination in 661. His followers deeply lamented his loss, but they also had to contend with the death of Ali's wife, the Prophet's daughter Fatima, and finally with the assassination of the two sons of Ali and Fatima, Hasan and Husayn. All of this blood permanently stained Islam, especially the Shiite tradition. The Shiites have kept lamentation over the fate of Ali, Fatima, Hasan and Husayn alive and central in their piety. Through the many eras when they were in the minority and subject to abuse by the Sunnis, remembering the rightness of their cause, the price that their martyrs had paid, and the sureness of God's coming to punish their enemies and reward them for their faith was the mainstay of Shiite strength.

Naturally there is much more one would have to narrate to give the full background of the Ayatollah Khomeini's decision in the case of the radio broadcast that called into question the adequacy of the Prophet's daughter Fatima as a role model for present-day Iranian women. Nonetheless, perhaps the force of his reaction now makes more sense. Knowingly or not, the woman who gave that doubting opinion put a match to a powder keg. Fatima has always been the prime role model for all Muslim women, but her close ties to Ali and Hasan and Husayn have made her especially beloved to the Shiites.

Moreover, Muslims in general and Shiites in particular have felt under attack in modern times. Often they have focused their resentment on the West, and a particular target of their ire has been what they have taken to be Western efforts to "liberate" Muslim women. The Ayatollah Khomeini came to power because he symbolized resentment of the Shah who, supported by the United States, had tried to modernize Iran. One of the Shah's modernizations was to remove some hindrances to women's education and full entry into Iranian cultural life--for example, the requirement that women wear the chador, the wrap-around clothing that had become traditional. The Ayatollah Khomeini's regime immediately reimposed the obligation to wear the chador, along with other symbols of traditional Muslim faith. To find such symbols challenged, especially in the form of a direct question about the adequacy of Fatima as a role model, must have sent the Ayatollah's blood pressure skyrocketing. Here again was blasphemy, heresy, outrage, effrontery. Here again was the critical, anti-religious mind of the West reaching into Iranian life, threatening the soul of what had made Iran great: its submission to Allah and his Prophet.

In the next section I shall deal with the psychology of a reaction such as the Ayatollah's and link it with the blood that the world religions so often have spilt tragically. Here let us pause to consider the general features of the story we have been following. For regularly it is the case that what one reads in the newspapers or sees on television has a fuller background than what the media present. Their space or time is limited, and frequently so is their knowledge. Almost always, some awareness of such a fuller background complicates the black and white assessment one is inclined to make. To be sure, no background can mitigate fully or excuse acts of savagery, but usually knowing more means sympathizing more, as well as being less surprised.

To switch to another world-famous religious authority, one might consider the background that makes Pope John Paul II's adamant opposition to birth control, as well as abortion, intelligible. For the religious culture in which John Paul II grew up, God had encoded into human nature certain inviolable laws. Among these was the orientation of sexuality to procreation. The interpretation of such laws finally lay in the hands of the leaders of the Christian Church, the pope and bishops. Such leaders were not free to change God's laws, because God's laws had a timeless dimension. At the least, therefore, Pope John Paul II was formed with a bias against arguments to the effect that changed relations between the sexes, or great increases in world population, meant one ought to rework one's sexual morality.

There is more, however, to the Pope's history and story. The traditional faith that he now feels charged to uphold was the mainstay of his Polish people through two nightmarish recent experiences. The Nazi occupation during World War II, and the Communist rule that the Soviets had imposed since World War II, both threatened traditional Polish culture (which already had a long history of sufferings). The main resource people had for resisting these threats was their longstanding Catholic faith, with its authoritarian, clerical character. If the Pope were to dilute this faith, he could feel he was turning his back on the way that God had saved the Polish people. Imagine the great pressure that would place on him to defend the inner precincts of traditional Catholicism with might and main.

Now, the history of both Islam and Catholic Christianity is vastly more complicated than what we have indicated in these two examples. And from that more complicated history come dozens of alternatives to the choices that the Ayatollah and the Pope have made. Many Muslims would not agree with the Ayatollah that rethinking the adequacy of Fatima as a role model means jettisoning a sacred tradition, let alone that it merits flogging or death. Many Catholic Christians think that natural law theory is outmoded and that Polish Catholicism, being far from the only tradition, ought not to have a monopoly on the influences shaping Church leaders. The stories we read in the newspapers, and the histories that lie in their background, finally suggest that all groups and individuals have to choose which aspects of their tradition they are going to emphasize on a given occasion. Is the severity of Allah going to weigh heavier than Allah's mercy? Is natural law going to weigh heavier than the freedom for which (Paul says in Gal. 5:1) Christ has set his followers free? These are the sorts of questions that open the possibility that much of the tragedy in religious history is unnecessary--chosen by people who might have known and done better.

2. Tragedy in the World Religions

If we take bloody religious war as a manifestation of the tragic potential in the world religions, it is clear that history affords us only too many sobering examples. Both within given religious traditions (Hinduism, Buddhism, Islam, Christianity) and between different traditions, the love of God or of holiness has often brought people to arms. Indeed, Muslims have spoken of the duty inscribed in the Qur'an to fight

67

against enemies of Allah, and this led the Ayatollah Khomeini not only to wage war against Iraq, whose people's Muslim faith he had criticized, but also to persecute such dissidents as Baha'is, calling them fighters against God. Christians have no reason to feel superior, because their history of religious warfare soiled the map of Europe, and Northern Ireland remains eloquent testimony that Protestant-Catholic hatred is far from dead. To be sure, the war between Iran and Iraq, like the conflict in Northern Ireland, is a complex phenomenon. Economic and cultural factors weigh at least as heavily as religious ones. The same is true of the crusades, Christian and Muslim, that wrought so much destruction in the Middle East, of the religious wars that followed on the Protestant Reformation, and of parallel conflicts in India (for example, the strife at the partition of Pakistan in 1947), China (for example, the persecution of Buddhists in 845), Africa, and other lands. Nonetheless, regularly people have tried to justify their warfare by appealing to God. Their fighting, they have claimed, was a holy cause, carried out for the defense and honor of their deity.

According to the Bible, ancient Israelites felt that they had been commissioned to wrest control of Canaan from its original inhabitants, and that God required the slaughter of such enemy infidels. One can see flickers of this mentality in Israel today. A solid core of those Israelis who oppose any concessions to the Palestinians claim that God gave the Holy Land to the Jews in perpetuity and that it is legitimate, if not admirable, to eliminate any interlopers threatening Israeli security. With a different historical background, but similar psychodynamics, Muslims and Christians have fought in Africa, Hindus and Muslims have fought in India, Christians and Muslims have fought in Soviet Armenia.

Common to all of these antagonisms, it seems, is a sense of election. Religious traditions, along with ethnic customs, language, and economic interests, have offered a basis for thinking that one's own kind had special rights, special sensitivities, and so special grievances when things went badly. Historically Christians persecuted Jews because Christians were offended that Jews would not accept Jesus as the Messiah, because Christians were in the majority and could do as they wished, because Jews were different and talented, because Christians wanted a scapegoat, and for God knows what other reasons. Central to all such persecution, however, was a Christian sense that faith in Jesus made Christians better than Jews-- indeed, better than all other peoples. Jews and Muslims both have had their own versions of such a sense of superiority and election. Jews have claimed to be the chosen people, God's own portion, and have relegated all non-Jews to the status of being merely "the nations" (goyim). Muslims have claimed that the revelations to Muhammad completed Judaism and Christianity and were superior.

On the whole, the Eastern traditions have not spoken so forcefully about election. Yet Buddhism often presented itself as a correction of the prior Indian tradition loosely summarized as "Hinduism," and in China Buddhists, Confucians, and Taoists often competed for supremacy aggressively, destructively. In Japan Shinto and Buddhism usually maintained an uneasy peace, punctuated by antagonism, whereas soon after Christianity came to Japan it was subject to fierce persecution. The modern era has seen Communist regimes proceed with what can only be called religious zeal against non-Communist faith: Christian, Jewish, Buddhist, Confucian, and other.

The identification of one's tradition, one's cause, one's people, or one's own authority as an Ayatollah or Pope with the righteousness of God scandalizes the modern mind and calls religion into question as deeply dangerous. That identification seems the special blindness of the world religions, when one considers their contributions to the world's measures of suffering. Not only has their militant righteousness brought millions of deaths in battle, it has also ridden roughshod over the consciences of individuals and taken away much of their joy. For example, the patriarchal world over women have heard the sermon that they have been made by God as the second sex, subordinate to men. Indeed, women have often heard the sermon that they are deeply flawed, because tempting to men. One consequence of their supposed flaw has been the concealing clothing women have been ordered to wear. Others have been women's rejection as unfit to serve at the altar as priests, to study Torah (divine instruction), to run their own Buddhist monasteries without interference from monks, and to gain release from what Hindus have called samsara (the realm of rebirth caused by karma). To escape karma, Hindu women would have to be reborn as men. Take the number of people afflicted by religious wars throughout history, add the number of women whose lives were blighted by religious patriarchies, and you will have a majority of the populations that have lived under the world religions. That seems like tragedy on a grand scale.

For, according to their own scriptures and ideals, the religions want to be ways of liberation, helps toward happiness. For example, the Buddha proposed his Four Noble Truths as a way to help people out of suffering. Jesus spoke about the Reign of God as a time and state when the justice never yet found on earth would finally prevail. Muhammad wanted to give his Arab people a source of unity and expose them to the splendid beauty of the Lord of the Worlds. Confucius thought that he was bringing to his troubled times, when strife was everywhere, the medicine of ancient wisdom that might heal them. For the high-minded, lofty, and indeed often effective ventures that followed in the wake of such great religious founders to have compounded human beings' sufferings so often is an enormous tragedy. What is it in the human makeup that makes election, arrogance, the attempt to equate the authority of religious leaders with the authority of God so recurrent a temptation? What do the history of religion and the psychology of the authoritarian religious personality tell us about sanity and health?

3. Toward Health and Sanity

In my opinion, as laid out in a textbook my husband and I have written on the world religions (The Story of World Religions [Menlo Park, CA: Mayfield, 1988], pp. 463-475), the stories of the world religions may be grouped into at least five different genres. Only one of these genres is tragedy. Many of the historical tales and literary products of the world religions better qualify as mysteries, or romances, or war stories, or comedies. Still, the tragedies, which often overlap with the war stories, furnish a great prod to think about all that has gone wrong. When I do, the deepest point I reach is the place where religious people are open or closed to the divine mystery. At what the mystics have called the ground or fine point of the soul, one either experiences the real transcendence of ultimate reality or one blocks off that experience and so deforms one's consciousness. This is a difficult as well as an important concept, so let me elaborate it.

It is one thing to say that God is transcendent, meaning by that that God goes beyond any words, concepts, doctrines, rituals, or ethical precepts in which human beings may try to express the divine. It is another thing to have experienced such transcendence—been shaken to the core by the realization that nothing that human beings can touch or think gives them surety, certainty, an archimedian point from which to lever the world. The same churches and synagogues and mosques that speak quite well of the transcendence of God, and so castigate idolatry on the left and human self-sufficiency ("works") on the right, so repeatedly fall into dogmatism, arrogance, and harshness toward the consciences of their adherents that one has to suspect they either have never been shaken by the transcendence of God or have forgotten that singular experience. (The parallel for Buddhists would be to speak about nirvana or emptiness yet become puritanical about sex or alcohol. The parallel for Taoists would be to confess the Tao that cannot be named yet get lost in religious rituals designed to harmonize the yin and yang forces of nature.)

When the personality, religious or secular, has not been formed by a profound realization that mystery and silence are more original and significant than insight and speech, it is on the verge of idolatry and arrogance. Certainly, human beings have to try to understand, to express their insights, and to sketch what behavior seems just, wise, and sanctifying. Certainly, they have to try to keep faith with revelations they believe have come to them through scriptures or the lives of their saints. But when they lose contact with the living presence of ultimate reality as a force or an order that escapes their comprehension, their doctrines, rituals, and ethical codes are in danger of reification. Reification is making a thing out of something that ought only to be an analogy or symbol. It is reading literally what by its nature has to be metaphorical. Every religion that has developed a strict legal code and tried to define sin and virtue in terms of disobedience or obedience to that code has regularly fallen into reification. At a sweep, that raises a major charge against Judaism, Christianity, and Islam, three prophetic religions

(religions deriving from revelations given to holy spokesmen) that ought to have known better than to canonize law. The analogies in the cases of Buddhism, Hinduism, Chinese religion, Japanese religion, and other traditions are not hard to find, because virtually everywhere human beings need to, and like to, make laws. (Secular societies are if anything worse, as the contemporary United States and USSR both suggest.)

Now, if we join this discussion with our previous reflections on chosenness and holy war, we find that many traditions have lost not only the humility and muteness that genuine experience of God inculcates but also the proper focus for religious zeal. To experience the awesome holiness of the power, the divinity, suggested by the Big Bang, by the intricacy of DNA, by the functioning of the human brain, by the birth of a child, by a Beethoven symphony, by the crucifixion of Christ, and even by such horrors as the Nazi holocaust of 6 million Jews is to come away consumed with the conviction that nothing is so important, so valuable, as the unnamable reality to which the most significant features of existence point and give access. Without that ultimate reality nothing would be or have any value, because everything depends upon that ultimate reality. Everything good and beautiful assumes it, and everything evil and ugly creates a cry in the human heart that that ultimate reality make things right. So the zeal of religious founders and saints makes great sense.

What does not make any truly religious sense is drawing from such zeal either reasons to inflate one's own importance or reasons for trying to compel, let alone abuse, other people. The experience of God intrinsically and inevitably makes one bow low and feel unworthy. That is the universal testimony of shamans, prophets, and sages. Interestingly, such "unworthiness" is objective rather than subjective. It is simply the proper response to the grandeur of the divinity or ultimate reality one has witnessed, somewhat the way that the smallness one feels when facing an ocean whipped by a hurricane is completely objective. The experience of God does not slash at one's proper self-confidence or self-love. Far from it. Rather, it gives one a reason to exult, to want to live and work, to cry out with joy and thanksgiving as no self-concern or elation over one's own achievements ever could. The best of human experiences--falling in love, receiving a fit of creativity--point in this direction. They too are not ego-inflating but humbling. They too come as a grace, a free gift, making one instinctively pray not to abuse them, to push ego and selfishness out of the way.

So, the crux of a religion's performance would seem to be its fidelity or infidelity to the experiences that formed it in the beginning and have to be assumed remain available every day. By my reckoning, the religions are very right to say that the only "solution" to humanity's many problems is finally an experience of transhuman reality that seems capable of transforming human nature. They are profoundly wise to say, with Saint Augustine, "You have made us for yourself, O God, and our hearts are restless till they rest in You." They have been healthy and sane to link this single overwhelming truth--all order in human affairs depends on openness to transcendence--with metaphors that might evoke it for newcomers, rituals that might tutor the senses and the heart in what transcendence feels like, sacraments that might suggest how the holiness of transcendence touches material things like bread and wine, and even models of the practical, ethical consequences that openness to transcendence, formation in conscience by transcendence, seems to indicate. Where they have failed regularly, and so most profoundly teach us about our own failings, is in having thought that their experiences of transcendence, great or small, gave them a basis for thinking themselves elect, or for riding out to slay infidels, or for pontificating about marital love, or for deciding to the point of harsh criminal sanctions what might be said about traditional role models. Each time the religions decline into such arrogance, they make us question the depth of their wisdom, the handle they have on their main business: the mystery of God.

Conclusion

Talk about the mystery of God is difficult. People want to hear it, because even the dullest suspect that life has to be more than money and banking, food and sex. Yet people also don't want to hear it, because God cannot be pinned down, because God threatens their securities, because God asks them to think harder and dig deeper into their hearts than they

73

are accustomed to doing. Ironically, and blessedly, the message of the world religions is that God, the ultimate reality, won't let us be as trivial, as lazy, as stunted as much in us wants to be. In a great mercy, God takes the pains of our lives, which are probably our major stimuli to reflection and spiritual growth, and makes them invitations to conversion: being turned in another direction, entertaining the at first seemingly crazy possibility that what meets the eye is the merest fraction of what is going on, what reality actually contains.

The story of the world religions is finally nothing but the story of human beings told from a particular angle. The Ayatollah Khomeini and Pope John Paul II are more like the rest of us than not--because they were born of women both thrilled and terrified, because they suffered as little children, because they need food and rest, because they know a few things and don't know many more. Every time they pray, they are invited to realize that their God is infinitely greater than they, making them like grains of sand along the seashore. Every time they defecate they are invited to realize they are just like all their brothers and sisters: bodily through and through, mortal, irremediably ignorant. There is no learning, no grant of authority, no title, no religious emotion that can take them outside the demands of their bodies for food, rest, and defecation. There is no perception of God that places God under their control. God always remains the initiator, the source of grace and wonders. They always remain the respondents, the seconders, the humble servants. And since God the initiator has shown them the mercy of drawing near for their comfort, through prayer or scriptures or sacraments, they have the obligation to comfort their brothers and sisters. The solidarity imposed on them by their bodies finds a parallel in the solidarity shown them in their souls. Everything is grace.

Nobody deserves God's favor. Any genuine experience of God is humbling and increases one's gratitude and love. Not to come away from prayer, religious study, or the exercise of one's religious office more kindly disposed toward one's brothers and sisters is to suggest, strongly, that one's religion has been false. Not to grow more aware of the mysteriousness of all things attending God, and so of all things significant about human beings, is to suggest that one is drifting or backsliding.

To be sure, the mercy of God is so rich that God has found ways of dealing with our religious falseness and backsliding. All the world religions talk about overcoming ignorance or sin, talk about enlightenment or redemption. God is the repair, as well as the creation and fulfillment, of our human natures. God has ways of redeeming the 50 lashes imposed by a bent Ayatollah, of smoothing the spiritual scars increased by an insensitive Pope. The Christian scripture says, "Even when our hearts condemn us, God is greater than our hearts" (I John 3:20). Not even our guilt, our rightful self-accusation, is the final word. Only God, the Tao, the Buddhanature, is the final word. If God is--and our experience that no thing is God suggests that God must be--then tragedy is not final. Comedy more befits us, and we should laugh at the religious leaders, as well as at the secular leaders, who take themselves so seriously that they think they can dictate our meaning. We should throw back our heads and say, "Thank God, no."

VII

VALUES IN THE CURRICULUM

I conceive my task in this chapter to be to offer
a useful, challenging perspective on what teachers
working in the tradition of liberal education should be
up to nowadays.   Let me approach this goal in three
unequal steps: first, a brief reflection on the
significance of the college curriculum; second, a
longer reflection on the value of a liberal education;
and third, a longer reflection on some of the specific
attitudes that I hope the sum of college courses in the
natural   sciences,   the   social   sciences,   and   the
humanities are communicating.

1.   The College Curriculum

As a veteran faculty member, with service at a
half-dozen different colleges or universities and some
time in departmental administration, I have found
discussion of the college curriculum to be a hardy
perennial, bound to pop up every spring (and many a
fall).   No doubt most such discussion is well-
intentioned, and no doubt it rests on the unassailable
proposition that it is good to have some rationale for
the academic programs one is packaging.

Nonetheless, I must confess to some fatigue from
the concern with curricular matters that I have
experienced.   In part, this fatigue comes from the
perception that faculty members seldom agree on the
best strategies for producing educated people, and that
occasionally they don't even agree on what constitutes
an educated person.   Indeed, a few times I have found
myself concluding that those most absorbed with

curricular reform were making what I judged to be a hash of the process because they themselves were not well educated.

A more intriguing aspect of this matter, however, may be another perception that I have come to respect, which is that what students study formally is less important than their falling in love with study itself. Naturally, this does not mean that I would be happy with a curriculum heavy on the history of the Baltimore crabcake or lenient with credits for volleyball. But it does mean that rather traditional divisions of required courses into such blocks as the natural sciences, the social sciences, and the humanities do not disturb me. Granted substantial courses that investigate questions customarily considered significant according to respected methodologies, I am most interested in catalyzing students with the experience that insight is self-fulfilling and self-justifying.

Further, I am keen on the idea that when the experience of insight is made central, education starts to unfold from the inside, intrinsically, as students realize that their next step ought to be to investigate the sources on which the author who shed light on their problem depended, or as they appreciate that what they learned in history is relevant to this problem they are pursuing in philosophy. At quixotic moments, I have even imagined designing a tutorial form of education in which students would begin by confessing what most interested them--music, business, athletics, romance, whatever--and well-educated teachers would come up with the first readings for what all hoped would unfold as a natural education based on following one's nose. The assumption would be that reality, and so learning, is sufficiently organic to allow one to begin, for example, with music and fairly easily come upon the relevance of mathematics, history, biology, and the rest. If the student were in fact passionate about music, and could be brought to understand something significant about music, then the doors would open and the next year's worth of work would stand revealed.

Since such a tutorial form of education will not usually be practical, much of my tactics has become accepting whatever layout of courses the curriculum of my school provides and trying, within that framework, to set up experience of understanding that will reveal interdisciplinary possibilities and so tell students how their education might become integral. In such an approach objective factors (one's sense of how the disciplines correlate, in terms of the questions they raise and how reality itself is best managed through categories) interweave with subjective factors (what this given student is interested in and can handle, whether the history professor has a better or worse reputation than the philosophy professor). Granted basic, minimally adequate coverage of the major methodologies and areas of reality, I tend to push students toward the courses most likely to engage them and provide significant experiences of insight. Better a third course in literature or chemistry that draws a student deeper into the love of learning than a nondescript second course in something that "curricular balance" might suggest.

2. The Value of a Liberal Education

Implicit in this discussion of the curriculum has been a commitment to an education that focuses more on the development of the individual student than on professional preparation. I realize that professional education is the fact in many situations, and that realists have to work within parameters set by facts. On the other hand, I believe that ideally professional education would follow after a basically liberal education, and that curricula are badly distorted when such a basically liberal education is not the driving force. Elitist as it may seem to some, I believe that business education, like education in law and medicine, ought to follow after studies in many things that many people in business might consider only marginal to their enterprise: natural sciences, social sciences, literature, history, philosophy, and religion. Unless such materials dominate a student's undergraduate work, someone has abdicated the principle that a college should be trying to educe or liberate the basic potential of the individual to grow lifelong in appreciating the wonders of creation, both natural and human. As well, a college has probably shown itself to be quite shortsighted, because without depth, breadth, and impracticality, an education is likely to be outmoded in five years.

This position regarding professional education implies that what people do to earn their bread is only part of what colleges are obliged to consider. While such a view is hardly novel, most teachers meet many students who do not accept the philosophy of education behind it, and many teachers have struggled with accreditors of professional educations--in business, engineering, or even (Lord help us) education--who have little patience with it. To the mind of some such accreditors, there can never be too many courses in accounting, or hydraulics, or classroom methods. Therefore, there can never be much "free" space for electives in literature or languages. So, mourning the pain it brings, one hears echoing from one's own exposure to the classics the old saying, "Who will take care of the caretakers?" In biblical terms, this is the problem of the eye growing dim and so the whole organism floundering in darkness. Brutally put, it is the burden many educators have to carry today because of the illiteracy not just of our students but, more horribly, of our comrades in the teaching ranks. With shrunken souls, they would diminish the whole of education to their own dwarfish stature. One can only resist them, with good arguments, kindness, and wicked satire, because they know not what they do and the wreckage they would strew is young people's lives.

From the sort of education that I advocate, which is broad, deep, and liberal, three values (in the sense of traits graduates ought to display) come to mind as worth receiving special attention. First, there is the valuable trait of the developed, critical mind. We pay lip-service to such a mind in our college catalogues, and we treasure it among our peers, but trying to nurture it in our students tries our patience, reminding us that despite their large size or apparent sophistication many of those sitting in front of us are woefully immature. Sometimes educators describe this immaturity as "a lack of conceptual skills." Ah, sweet mystery of professional language! I believe they mean to say that the kids don't think very well. In some cases there is little one can do, since thinking well is a direct correlative of intelligence. As Bernard Lonergan, my mentor in cognitional theory, said somewhat sardonically, "Insight is the act that occurs frequently among the intelligent and rarely among the stupid."

In other cases, the problem is less a matter of native talent than of bad education to date. Without castigating primary and secondary schooling, the problems of which can make the college campus seem like

Eden, we have to face the fact that many of our students come having had little exercise in close reading, or the quick manipulation of figures, or memorization, or analysis, or logic, or writing, or precise speaking. Their vocabularies are embarrassingly limited, and often they turn truculent when forced to use a dictionary, so foreign a venture would that be. If they cannot understand "it" when they begin, "it" must be hopelessly difficult or irrelevant, and so the teacher propounding "it" and requiring that "it" be mastered is a tyrant, or a bully, or some other species of taskmaster manifestly unfair.

It's not clear how one should factor into one's analysis of this state of affairs the influence of television, videos, and the other aspects of our return to an oral culture, or to a visual culture not focused on books. It remains true that there is no frigate like a book, but how many students know what a "frigate" is, or why Emily Dickinson might be considered heroic as well as neurotic, or what venturing through mental universes entails? Whatever the causes, the fact, as I see it reflected in the puzzled frowns of many of my students, is that most of them don't handle language, even their native English, very well. Other teachers will have to speak about quantitative skills, but every time I have to do the simple math for my checkout person at the supermarket I'm not encouraged to think that math is faring any better than English.

Thus, aspiring to develop critical reason-- disciplined, honed intelligence--in one's students means getting in there with a lot of pointed questions, to siphon away the fog, to replace a lot of flab with some muscle, and to make students aware, often for the first time, that words are referential and that good thought requires evidence, premises, and a logical march to conclusions. Knowledge maketh a bloody entrance, even when it is not dragged up from the roil of deep emotions. If students do not come to us able to handle ideas, we have to see them through a painful process that is much like the birth of a mind. For that reason, no doubt, Plato thought of education as a midwifery.

The second value that I would stress in liberal education is compassion, which I see as the affective

equivalent of critical intelligence. We discipline the
mind to sharpen its understanding and prepare good
judgment. However, unless we educate the imagination
and emotions as well, good judgment will remain
rationalistic, detached, less potent and effective in
the realms of politics, family life, ecology, and
religion than it might and should be. But how does one
develop compassion? How does one so educate students
that they feel solidarity with the suffering and can
articulate their outrage at injustice? A good
question. The college or university is not a
counseling center, desirable though it be that colleges
and universities have counseling centers. The college
or university also is not a church, synagogue, or
mosque, desirable though it be that colleges and
universities respect and forward authentic religious
values. So the main vehicle for the college or
university's development of healthy affections such as
compassion has to be precisely educational: something
prosecuted in the classroom, in study assignments, in
library research. My sense is that this best occurs
when we make compassion, and other desirable
affections, a factor in the books we choose for our
reading lists, the topics we assign for our term
papers, and the questions toward which we turn class
discussions.

For example, when I teach my regular course on the
New Testament and Literature, or on Women and World
Religions, I am always looking for readings that render
the familiar texts or the formal doctrines personally
gripping. My assumption is that the teachings of
Jesus, or the views of the Buddha, or the rituals that
Hindu women have used to pace themselves through the
life-cycle originally were very gripping, and that they
remain gripping for ardent Christians, Buddhists, or
Hindus today. "Gripping" is hardly a precise word, but
certainly it implies that the values being communicated
have holistic effects. The original, creative
Christian, Buddhist, and Hindu educations traded in
images that purported to change people's sense of
reality, in ceremonies designed to draw initiates more
deeply into the mysteries being celebrated by engaging
all of their senses, in community bondings that stirred
warmth, fellow-feeling, and sympathy. Through the
books I select, the films I use, the way I slant my
lectures, and the rest of my pedagogical repertoire, I
try to render something of this holism and affectivity.
I attempt this both as an act of fidelity to the

tradition we are studying and as an effort to stir students to imagine and feel in themselves some values that might be equivalent in their own cultures.

Clearly, religious studies is a field in which it is not difficult to work out ways to suggest affective virtues, but I suspect that teachers of literature, history, philosophy, political science, and classical studies can manage analogous strategies fairly easily. So, I suspect, can teachers of the social sciences, whenever they let the personal impact of organizational forms, or psychological development, or economic policies, or anthropological insights have some say. For the natural sciences, I think of books that mediate the joy of discovery, or the appreciation of nature's complexity, or the outrage that pollution can incite. In fact, few of us college teachers got into our disciplines without considerable emotional excitement and investment. In fact, most of us have sensed how what we study and teach might be highly relevant to making the world a place more fit to live in. With a little imagination, we ought to be able to show our students some of this passion and its objective causes, and then to correlate it with the pathos of the finite, mortal, suffering condition all human beings share.

I can foresee two further questions about targeting a value such as compassion, so I feel obliged to allude to both at least passingly. The first question is whether getting involved with the affective or the emotional does not muddy the waters and deflect professors from the intellectual center of their project as college educators. The reply, both obvious and finally a matter of ostensive rather than strictly reasoned definition, is that our students are not minds but whole personalities, that history and reality are wholes including not only ideas but also much emotion and force, and so that if we are to deal with either our students or our subject matter adequately we have to incorporate the affective dimension.

The second question, which I'll break into two parts, is why I single out compassion and how I would nurture it. I single out compassion because it seems to lie at the foundations of the social outlook I want to encourage and to translate much of the basic commandment, articulated by Jesus but available in other places (for example, in Confucian tradition), that we are to love our neighbors as ourselves. I think that the surest foundation of such a love is the instinct singled out by the Chinese sage Mencius: jen (fellow-feeling, spontaneous sympathy). Mencius gives the example of a child crawling toward an open well. Virtually anyone, stranger as much as mother, would rush to stop the child from falling in. When we let ourselves see the vulnerability and danger of the people around us, it is not hard to feel compassion and a desire to help. Should not a prime criterion of a liberal, liberating, education be whether it helps us let ourselves see the need and pain of the people around us?

How best to nurture compassion? My current bias is that the more we meditate on human mortality, letting the sureness of death assume in our philosophies the importance that arguably it should, the easier we will find it both to consider compassion highly relevant and to bring compassion into our syllabi. This bias lately has been fed by assignments to lecture on AIDS and abortion, but in the past I have had it triggered by discussions of the Holocaust, of apartheid, of turmoil in the Church, of victims of corporate takeovers and toxic dump sites. Any place that human beings are suffering is a place where compassion applies, and such places are obviously legion. The root of such suffering is our human vulnerability, which is rooted in our mortality. Because we all have to die, we all have a good reason to become compassionate.

The third virtue that I would want the curriculum of a liberal arts college to foster is faith. In part this is due to the character of many American colleges as founded to spread and nourish faith, but only in part. Faith has many analogues in the worlds of science, business, and the arts. The Pre-Socratics knew about faith, hope, and love, seeing them as virtues fundamental to spiritual maturity. For example, unless human beings can trust the existence into which they have been thrust, can share it openly with other people, can expect that it can have a good future, and can embrace it warmly, they can't be said to enjoy good mental health. Most teachers believe that they have an obligation to promote good mental health, through both their curricular materials and their general attitudes. Frequently this is something they need not advert to explicitly. Frequently their own joy, energy, or willingness to slug through hard times make it plain that they are carried by faith. But on the occasions when course materials verge upon the depths of human existence, or upon the questions of the Beginning and the Beyond, or upon the problem of human twistedness or upon the dysfunctions in either nature or society, faith may come into explicit focus. Then we have the delicate but one hopes welcome task of showing both the reasons and the more than rational bases for going on--for gambling that it does all make sense, for opening our hearts to what is beautiful and not shying away from what is ugly, for finally commending our spirits into a mystery we trust will be parental.

At this point, I am obviously close to something about which specifically Christian faith has been eloquent. In Pauline terms, faith is a matter of thinking that to live is Christ and to die is gain. In Johannine terms, faith is a matter of abiding with a presence one believes is the community of Spirit, Son, and Father. Perhaps only theology courses have many occasions to speak in trinitarian terms, but the Trinity is the font of many experiential analogies. Whenever we trust that light, life, and love are primordial goods, we commit ourselves to the mystery that Christian faith says is wholly good and communitarian. Whenever we sense that honesty and love are the hallmarks of integrity and maturity, we embody the venerable tradition that human beings are images of God, and that through their most human acts divinity is making them partakers of its own deathless life of perfect knowing and loving. An education offered under Christian auspices that did not mine such riches would be defaulting on a great potential. When critical intelligence and compassion join with a sense of living within the contours of the paschal mystery, one has the best of Christian liberal educations.

3. Values Germane to Particular Curricular Areas

In this section I want to assume what I said about the primacy of helping students to fall in love with learning, and about the worth and ideal effects of a liberal education generally, moving into some suggestions about the values that studies of nature, society, the self, and God can inculcate. This will involve some overlap with the prior discussion of critical intelligence, compassion, and faith, but on the whole I shall be stressing the fairly objective response that I believe each of the primal zones of being solicits. I might mention that I borrow this fourfold delineation of reality--nature, society, self, and divinity--from Eric Voegelin, author of the monumental <u>Order and History</u> (Baton Rouge: Louisiana State University Press, 1956-87), who has served me as a wonderful model of the breadth and depth that the intellectual life can nourish.

Courses in the natural sciences trade on the wonder that Aristotle placed at the foundations of the love of wisdom. No doubt this wonder can get lost in the paraphernalia of the laboratory, but I suspect that happy scientists are always drawing upon it. Humanists such as I depend on a Stephen Hawking to communicate the nearly incredible reaches of the universe, in both its macro-features and its micro-features. I tend to get my sense of the stunning beauty and complexity of physical life from a Lewis Thomas or a Barry Lopez, who takes medical knowledge or field biology as a stimulus for meditation about the build of natural reality. But surely those who deal with mathematics and physics, with chemistry and biology, on a professional basis can make cognate points with their students regularly. Surely the intrigue of the physical world, its amenability to rational investigation, ought to sponsor an abiding respect for its role in our mental as well as our physical well-being. We are creatures designed to raise questions, programmed by nature to want to know. Few enterprises can rival modern science in the success of its response to this want, so any course in the natural sciences is fertile territory for implanting a lifelong fascination with how things came into being and now work.

In addition to fostering the virtue or value of wonder, the natural sciences might also target a particular species of compassion. The data on what we human beings have been doing to the vulnerable earth that is the matrix of our life are now so compellingly disturbing that the morality of our technological way of life deserves serious scrutiny. If the earth cannot sustain our present patterns of population growth, deforestation, water pollution, air pollution, pollution of the earth with toxic chemicals, and the like, our present patterns in the industrialized northern nations bear a heavy burden of proof. At the least, those most informed about the impact of human interventions into the environment have the

86

opportunity, and probably the responsibility, to make plain what we are doing. Whether or not they agree that what we are doing amounts to geocide or matricide, they certainly have a wonderful opportunity, by the example of their own attitude toward the physical world as well as their formal remarks, to teach students the value of treating the earth as a precious endowment, something we did not create and so have no right to deface or destroy.

In the social sciences, the value of compassion seems intimately tied to the value and virtue of justice. The social sciences deal with how human beings live together. When human beings live together sharing both burdens and benefits fairly, society prospers, even in difficult circumstances. Economists have at their fingertips both global and domestic statistics translating the monied aspects of social justice. They can find out, with little difficulty, how income varies in the American population, or by comparison of the American and the Indian populations, providing an important factor in the calculations our whole race has to make about the fairness necessary for survival. Political scientists in league with economists can estimate the correlations between economic disparities or injustices and political turmoil. The dovetailing of land policies, income, and militant movements in Latin America, for example, seems a natural item to investigate. The voting patterns of Americans in different economic groups, as in different ethnic, religious, and geographical groups, are similarly suggestive of the connection between how people relate to what ought to be their commonweal and how they currently think about their share in the overall cornucopia of their society.

I am not going to labor to think up what may well be banal similar examples for teachers of sociology, psychology, or anthropology. Suffice it to say that these disciplines often work along potentially fascinating borders where how people treat one another is shown to depend on a variety of social factors. If our courses dealing with such factors do not strengthen our students' critical perception of the difficulties attending the creation of a just, happy, prosperous society, they have missed a great opportunity to inculcate judgmental rigor. Equally, if they have not strengthened our students' commitments to social justice, we may ask how valuable they are in the final analysis.

It is no secret that those proposing a dimension of social responsibility to students, or practitioners, in such fields as business and law can run into stiff opposition nowadays. One member of our Law faculty at the University of Tulsa recently described to us how he was hooted at a regional meeting for suggesting that corporations have responsibilities to more than the bottom line of their stockholders' profits. Frequently the greed supported by both substance and symbol during the Reagan administration lodges, almost touchingly, in our more ambitious students as a prime energy of the commendable life. Whenever we help sublate such energy into a broader vision of the commendable life, a vision more in keeping with human solidarity the world over, we do very good work.

The disciplines that bear on the self are many and varied, and of course they cannot rightly separate the self from its historical, social, or biological contexts. For brevity's sake, however, let me limit my remarks to the opportunities that I see such humanistic studies as literature and philosophy having to promote a rich love of the embodied self. Literature that helps us warm to our bodies, especially in their sexual complementarity, and that illustrates the mistakes we typically make, can do wonders for students' sense of self. Recently I have been impressed by Rosemary Haughton's use of the rise of Romance in the medieval period as an entry to the mysteries of the love attendant on the Incarnation of the Divine Word. The novellas of Andre Dubus amount to a stunning examination of what we have done to marriage and family life, where so much of our sense of self is shaped. Anne Tyler, working her Baltimore neighborhoods, is a wonderful exponent of the odd, the quirky, the angular ways that the complexities of selfhood slip out. Even John Updike, skating gracefully on the surface of upper-middle class self-indulgence, ends up teaching us much about love's labors lost. In philosophy, the Ricoeurs, Wittgensteins, and Heideggers, who teach us so much about language and symbolism, can elucidate the treasures of our embodied spirituality to similarly good effect. So much neurosis, and therefore social misfiring, stems from a lack of proper self-love that few virtues seem better targets for humanistic educators.

Last, concerning divinity, I would urge all the disciplines that deal with the traces God has left everywhere to consider the contemplative mind-set that tends to bring them their best appreciations of such traces, and to do what they can to encourage their students' contemplative potential. Whereas for theological studies this might entail some discussion of prayer proper, for many other disciplines it merely demands attending to the reflection, the musing, the shift from analysis toward synthesis and holism that sets the spirit free to develop the second naivete associated with wisdom. Divinity present everywhere as the mystery in which we live and move and have our being demands a holistic, contemplative response, because we can never match our minds to its infinity. To appreciate how it lingers in questions about why the Big Bang ever happened, or what the bloody travail of natural history and social history implies, or how creative artists come to their visions, or what moves parents when they comfort their children in the dark of night is to let go of one's regular categorizing and attend to a simple, seamless whole.

Eric Voegelin accepted the designation "mystic philosopher" because he realized that the order of history escapes the positivistic, perhaps even the critically realistic, mind. One has to muse one's way down the linguistic trail to get to the experiences of Israelite revelation and Greek philosophy that he thought structured Western history. One has to sense how the divine mystery forms the human spirit to health, if one is to appreciate the deformations worked by the modern gnosticisms. An education that does not nourish our contemplative wellsprings, showing us how there is more in our depths, as well as in the external world, than the pundits of the news media dream, is only half a loaf. The whole loaf, the education that gives full value, regularly trades in the fare that Lady Wisdom provides in the Book of Proverbs. With God when he playfully ordered the universe, she sets a table for all who would be educated by that realistic ordering, bidding the simple to taste her wares and leave off their simplicity, their ignorance of the splendors of God's creation.

Surely that is a good image to keep in mind as we prepare our students for graduation: have their years with us helped them toward an initial appreciation of the splendors of God's creation? Has their curriculum, the "course" they have run, made God's love, which is the "reason" for God's creation, their pearl of great price and highest value? I can only urge all educators who want their students to graduate with such values to keep up the good work, trusting that educating the young toward contemplative maturity and responsible citizenship is an extraordinarily high vocation.

VIII

VALUES IN HONORS EDUCATION

I have been involved with honors programs at both Wichita State University and the University of Tulsa. At both schools the talent and eagerness of the typical honors student have gladdened many teachers' hearts. For while a good teacher's heart certainly is moved by the student who has troubles, only overcoming such troubles is gladdening. When students are well-prepared and talented, more of the delight that ought to characterize higher education can emerge. As a consequence, the self-validating character of learning is not hard to prove. Honors students naturally have their own problems of discipline and motivation, but on the whole they have a good chance to make their own Aristotle's observation that all people by nature desire to know.

It is this desire that excellent education reverences and serves. When students have appropriated an excellent education, dicta such as Aristotle's are nothing extrinsic or formalistic. Rather they are home truths, exegeses of a core component of self-knowledge. And self-knowledge, as I don't have to remind you (but can't resist doing so), was the great command of the oracle at Delphi. When we know that we are made to know, and are made to love, we have in hand the anthropological wisdom that is the pearl of great price. Thenceforth, if we wish, we can dedicate our time to the spiritual life--the life of learning, prayer, love, and service that savants and saints alike witness is the grand realization of human potential.

Let me put some flesh on the skeletal topic "Values in Honors Education" by pursuing three issues:

91

the basic realms of reality that an honors education ought to explore and bring students to treasure, an experimental curriculum worth considering, and the freedom requisite for the best results in honors education. I assume that it will be clear that the entirety of my discussion of these topics bears on values, so only occasionally will I pause for an explicit reminder.

1. Values in the Basic Realms of Reality

Over the years I have found it useful in teaching courses in philosophy, religious studies, or the humanities to offer students a four-fold delineation of reality. This four-fold delineation, which I borrow from the philosopher of history and consciousness Eric Voegelin, considers nature, society, the self, and divinity irreducible zones or dimensions of the way things are, the way reality presents itself. Few analysts, East or West, would dispute the reality or utility of the first three differentiations. Nature is obvious, and although human beings clearly are immersed in nature, psychologically as well as biologically, the realms of culture that human beings contribute to the universe (the noosphere that Teilhard de Chardin stressed) arguably deserve considerable treatment as something distinguishable from nature. These realms of culture carry the tension between the individual and the group, the person and the society or community, and by consensus, common sense, and solid philosophical analysis one can make the case that the individual cannot be reduced or dissolved into the group, and that social dynamics are more than the mathematical sum of psychic dynamics. Thus to speak of nature, society, and the self as distinct realms raises few hackles.

The fourth realm, divinity, receives no contesting and much attention in all premodern cultures, but since the Enlightenment it has been problematic. This is not the place for a disquisition on theology, natural or revealed. Suffice it to say that for Voegelin, and for me, the perennial testimony of humankind to experiences of transcendent--more than natural, social, or psychic--reality is persuasive. Minimally, we are wise to heed this testimony when we read texts or examine artifacts from cultures in which divinity--the sacred, the numinous--is taken seriously. For example, to read the Bible or try to estimate its place in American culture without openness to the possibility that divinity is as real as death and healing, as stars and hospitals, is to make a hash of one's interpretation. Maximally, we are wise to consider the relevance of mystery, in the strict sense of a surplus of intelligibility, a riches beyond what finite human intelligence will ever master, to current cosmology, studies of history, and analyses of personhood.

Now, granted your acceptance of the viability of this fourfold scheme, or your cordial suspension of disbelief, let me indicate what we should expect an honors education to bring students to appreciate in each of the realms.

In the realm of nature, where the physical sciences obviously carry most of the load but humanists also ought to pay attention, the innate human desire to know has proven wonderfully productive. The world now sketched for us by astrophysicists, nuclear physicists, and geneticists, to speak only of specialities currently considered sexy, is (to borrow a phrase from Robertson Davies) "a world of wonders." It seems to me that the genius of modern science has been to tie the wonder through which we explore so challenging a universe to the strictest canons of intellectual discipline. Responding to a form of the mind's own hunger to refine itself and grow, as well as to the demands of natural phenomena, modern science has clarified the requirements of judgment--saying whether something is or is not likely to exist in such and such a form, according to such and such a pattern. Judgment, arguably, is the rite of passage to maturity. All those who have senses and minds in good working order have experience. Those who have curious, bright minds have understanding--insights that suggest hypotheses. But only the mature have good judgment: the self-criticism, the finessed awareness of our inbuilt requirements for sufficient reason (evidence and logic), that makes hypotheses more than bright ideas, moving us from the world of what might be so to the world that we can rely upon.

So, our honors students ought to come away from studies of nature with both a greatly deepened appreciation of the wonder of the physical world--its intricacy, vastness, depth, and change--and a greatly deepened appreciation of what the physical sciences and mathematics demand of the human mind, how they indicate the human mind ought to mature. An honors student not awed by nature and sobered by the challenges of the physical sciences that most directly explore nature is a student we have failed.

For the social sciences, the disciplines most directly concerned with the realm of society, the wonders stimulating the natural human desire to know probably cluster around such matters as how people tend to organize themselves, how they develop symbol-systems to carry and excite meaning, and why they suffer so many dysfunctions, beget so much war and suffering. Naturally we should encourage social scientists to make our students aware of the impact of nature on the technology, economics, health care, diet, art, and science of any given people. The realms of reality, and our studies of them, should not be sealed off from one another. In non-faddish ways, we ought to encourage honors students, especially, toward interdisciplinary work. But for the moment let me concentrate on the studies of sociologists, political scientists, some historians, anthropologists, some psychologists, economists, and the like whose main interest is neither the impress of nature nor the idiosyncrasies of individuals but the social behavior of human groups. What ought our honors students to take away from time spent with them?

I would nominate an appreciation of the complexities and riches of this realm analogous to the wonder I hoped studies of nature would create, and an analogous appreciation of the demands that social studies make on those who would prosecute them responsibly. The wonder is a response to the objective factor—the singing, dancing, building, buying and selling, educating, ruling, and myriad other enterprises through which human beings organize themselves, defend themselves, feed themselves physically and spiritually. The appreciation of what gaining clarity, realism, about such enterprises requires of the investigator is the subjective correlative, the entry-point for teachers wanting to stress the trickiness of language, statistics, archives, interviews, and all our other ways we have of mediating the data of human groups, both foreigners and fellow-citizens, to our own brains and those of the people we would instruct.

If we give the humanities the primary responsibility for studying the self not reducible to either its natural or its social aspects or components, we can note the function of literary studies, language studies, some historical studies, philosophy, religious studies, some disciplinary studies in communications, and no doubt many of the arts (music, painting) in elucidating individual creativity, suffering, self-expression, groping for existential meaning, love, faith, and much more. If the division between the impact of nature and the impact of groups is often shaky and artificial, clearly the division between humanistic approaches to experience and culture and approaches from the social sciences often is even more shaky and artificial. Though humanists on the whole are more interested in the individual than are social scientists, humanists also have to be greatly interested in groups--their movements, their narratives, their formation of individuals through rituals and educational schemata.

One of the first appreciations that I would hope honors students would bring away from their humanistic studies is the constant impress of historical period and social circumstances. Helpful as textual studies that focus on the intercourse between reader and particular text may be, it seems to me folly to neglect the historical and social circumstances of the author, let alone what we know about the individuality of the author from sources outside a particular text. Second, I would hope that students would gain a great appreciation of the variety of human experiences, choices, worldviews, and the like. The humanities ought to make the most cogent case they can for the human freedom that most cultures have accorded their citizens, if only in the form of holding them responsible for their crimes and misdemeanors.

If a student has not encountered the mysteriousness of artistic or literary creativity, the wonders of human love, the mental or spiritual component in truly human suffering, the ecstatic experiences that shamans, prophets, sages, and mystics have treasured beyond compare, and whatever other factors one would nominate as capital for grasping what an ineffable thing it is to be human, we teachers have failed again, this time egregiously. Self-knowledge, the high value of which I cited at the outset, depends on rich exposure to the fathomless, ineffable character of human nature--to all the paradoxes in the ancient view that human beings are unique for having to become what they are. For both the objective goal of appreciating human culture and selfhood, and the subjective goal of maturing a sensitive interpreter of human artifacts, such exposure, brought to reflective and critical clarity in the classroom, is nonpareil. Honors students exposed to challenging courses in the humanities ought to stream forth into our culture well-defended against the cant and manipulation that advertisers and politicians want to work upon them.

I have suggested that the realms of nature, society, and the self are all relevant to each of the main disciplinary areas--the natural sciences, the social sciences, and the humanities (and arts). The same is true of the fourth realm, divinity. Astrophysics, genetics, anthropology, and classical literature all raise questions about the source of order in the natural and moral realms. All vector toward experiences of transcendence that shamans and yogins, prophets and sages, have claimed disclose such a source. Nonetheless, religious studies most directly consider the divine reality, so in the measure we think it important for honors students to have a fully rounded education we will encourage them to do some religious studies.

The objective factor that honors students should encounter in such studies is the mysteriousness into which all our significant chains of questions take us. For example, the student studying the biology of aging often wonders about what causes death, how death is encoded in the genes of living things. This can lead to questions about death itself, the experience and the necessity. The term of such an inquiry only two or three steps removed from the initial wonder about the little bird on its back with its legs up rigid, concerns how creation finally is constructed and why mortality is so central to its design. But this is not a question one can answer empirically or by recourse to rational analysis alone. Yet all cultures have raised this question, and all cultures have tried to contain its debilitating effects through myths, rituals, and symbols that might guide people's hearts beyond where their minds can travel. Students who don't know about these questions and strategies come away with a truncated and so crippling sense of the objective world.

Subjectively, the study of divinity ought to increase the contemplative capacity of our students, making them familiar with the zones of their own awareness that are neither sensual nor intellectual. Such foreign cultures as those of India, China, and the medieval West, Christian and Jewish alike, did a better job on this matter than we modern or post-modern Westerners tend to do. Distraction and empiricism have made destructive inroads into our students' capacities to meditate or contemplate, so few of our students know much about the silence from which the most poetic speech proceeds, the darkness in which divinity tends to shroud itself, the background or horizon of consciousness that is both necessary for our knowing or loving any particular thing and the area where the constant presence of divinity (more intimate to us than we are to ourselves, Augustine claimed) is most likely to be experienced. If students have never been exposed to contemplation, can we consider them fully educated?

2. An Experimental Curriculum

I have skimmed over the four basic realms of reality, suggesting some of the values that a good honors education would inculcate. Let me now consider a specific proposal for the reworking of the traditional college curriculum, using it as a prod to question how our best students are likely to need to think about the world in the twenty-first century. The assumption of this specific proposal, like my assumption in the first section of this chapter, is that college experience ideally focuses on liberal education, leaving specialized or professional education to a post-graduate phase. Undergraduate education in business, nursing, education, and the like obviously would have to adapt both my general discussion of values in the realms of reality and the specific curricular proposal that I now treat.

The proposal is not my own. It comes from Thomas Berry, a man with background in Asian studies and ecology, and it may be found in the Winter 1989 issue of the journal Religion & Intellectual Life. Berry's thesis is that the best focus for an education that would integrate the most vital of our present data and prepare our students for the phase of world history currently emerging is the earth itself. In Berry's view, as long as we continue to neglect how the earth shapes human consciousness and human consciousness serves the earth as the organ through which it becomes aware of itself, we are unlikely to achieve "any adequate sense of what education is, or what a college is, or what an American college should be doing. This question [of how we ought to be educating our people] identifies with the question of what the earth is, what it is doing presently, and what are its directions in the future. Human intelligence is primarily the activation of the possibilities of the planet in a way that could not be achieved apart from human intelligence and the entire range of human activities. In this sense human education is part of the larger evolutionary process" (pp. 9-10).

Berry goes on to explain how he believes the earth has stimulated the rise of human consciousness, through genetic coding, and what larger context (the origin of the universe) the phases of cosmic history that have unfolded on the earth require for their best understanding. Then he outlines a series of courses that might communicate an adequate vision of how cosmic history has unfolded and where it now stands. It was these courses that caught my attention and triggered the idea of offering you a specific proposal. The six courses that Berry sketches as an adequate core curriculum would deal with: 1) the evolution of the cosmos in four phases (the formation of the galaxies, the formation of the earth within the solar system, the emergence of life upon earth, and the rise of human consciousness and cultural development); 2) the major phases in the history of human consciousness: the tribal-shamanic phase, the neolithic village, the period of the great religious cultures, the modern phase of science and technology, and the ecological phase that is currently emerging; 3) the classical cultures, East and West, that developed the majority of the ideas and values we still live by; 4) the scientific-technological phase of history, showing in some depth how we have come to our present awareness of the history--the time sequence or evolutionary unfolding--of the cosmos; 5) the age that is dawning or emerging, in which the interrelationship, the ecology, of all the components of the earth would be the focus and students might rethink the significance of such activities as law, medicine, religion, and commerce in this new context; 6) values, stressing such major features of the earth that has evolved as the uniqueness of each unrepeatable, irraplaceble articulation of reality (star, atom, bird, human being, whatever), the subjective, interior, or depth dimension of each reality, and the law of communion or interrelationship that binds all of the members of the earth together.

I have given only a quick digest of Berry's curricular proposal, but it has been dense enough to suggest the need for review. The guiding idea is to take the current stage of the earth, at which we human beings (the "mind" of the earth) let the whole realize how it has evolved to date and where it seems to be going, and make it the pivot of our educational venture. The argument, in other words, is that adequate education nowadays requires us to teach in a global context and with a reshading of all our prior intellectual horizons, based on such globalness. The specific core courses comprise a pattern of movement from the most general or overarching to the more specific. The first course is a macro-history: from the big bang to the present phase of global history. For Berry this macro-history has four main states: universal (before the formation of the solar system and the earth), the formation of the earth, the rise of life, and the rise and development of consciousness.

The second core course is an overview of the history of consciousness or culture: from tribal beginnings, through village life and civilization, through a modernity shaped by science and technology, to a current, post-modern phase characterized by ecological awareness (consciousness of interrelationship). The third core course directs attention to the phase of the great civilizations, East and West. The fourth core course directs attention to the modern period shaped by science and technology. The fifth core course directs attention to the current ecological period. And the sixth core course focuses on the main values that the entire process of cosmic history ought to lead us to prize: variety, interiority, and communion.

To Berry's mind, such a core curriculum would situate our students realistically, showing them the context in which they now have to think, if they are to embrace the expanse of what really exists. It would also give them the beginnings of an accurate, detailed understanding of how the planet that is their matrix, and whom (inevitably in Berry's perspective the earth becomes somewhat personalized) they serve as the apparatus for self-knowledge, has evolved--the main phases, with their characteristics, gains, and losses. Finally, Berry's core curriculum would clarify what has been most important, most to be prized and safeguarded, in the experience of the earth's evolution. Along the way, it would also shed new light on the global function of the many sub-processes ingredient to the whole history: for example, the biology of plants, the role of business, religious rituals, the steam-engine, current ecological pollution, or anything else one might name.

Now, I am not writing as a disciple of Thomas Berry, intent to preach a gospel of educational liberation through a conversion to ecology. My interest is rather to shake up the categories in which I usually hear education, including that for honors students, discussed and strike out for a more adequate vision. My assumption is that an education is valuable in the measure that the vision structuring it is wise and profound. Inevitably, we design according to our sense of the whole and the value of its parts. Few of the core curricula that I have studied have a central focus so precise, innovative, radical, and profound as Berry's, so I find his set of six courses intriguing. In fact, Berry offers many more specific suggestions for how to develop an earth-centered curriculum and how to exploit the escape from chauvinist cultural biases such a curriculum offers than space allows me to indicate. What at first appears radically new is at many points simply a repositioning of such traditional studies as the natural and social sciences, the history of civilizations, the story of modern science, and the ethical questions set us by ecological problems. The exciting feature is the fresh look we are likely to give many of our traditional and current concerns, because of their new context--Berry's stress on their interaction and subservice of the history and prospering of the earth. Whatever one thinks of Berry's proposal (and the respondents that the editor of <u>Religion & Intellectual Life</u> commissioned to criticize his article have many caveats), it has the great virtue of trying to bring to a core future education the full range of historical consciousness that our scientific and historical studies now allow us to glimpse.

3. Freedom in Honors Education

I shall treat my third topic comparatively briefly, not because it does not deserve leisurely study, but because my space is drawing to an end and I have already implied much of what I want to say about intellectual freedom. For example, I believe that honors education is wise to attempt a balance between the content traditionally associated with liberal education and new approaches or packagings that reflect the new stage of historical consciousness and planetary culture that we have reached. Unless educators and students are left free to exploit the resources of both the disciplines that have served liberal education well in the past and the new questions and answers that have come with recent gains in global awareness, they will be left with the unacceptable alternative of offering either an education solid but outmoded or an education truly contemporary but deracinated, faddish.

Second, I believe that honors students should be encouraged to make intellectual inquiry, and so academic freedom, the great value they personally serve in their study. Curricula come and go. Some are better and some worse. All, however, are instrumental--patterns meant to serve. But what are they meant to serve? Obviously, students' intellectual maturation. How in fact do we grow genuine intellectuals, people who will leave our schools prepared to study and expand their horizons for the rest of their lives? By seducing them, so that they fall in love with learning. If we can occasion enough experiences of understanding, enough times when the light flashes and students say, "Aha," we will have done what educators can to generate genuine intellectuals. Against the pragmatic biases strong in all historical periods, we will have established the justification for research, disinterested analysis, the contemplative life, study and creative expression.

Insight is self-validating. Once one has mastered the skills of learning, so that one can read, write, and compute well, the major problems become those of focus and time. There is so much to learn that we all need help to focus on what is most significant or best matches up with our own creativity. I suggest that those who have what Cardinal Newman called "the habit of philosophy" are well-positioned to offer advice on what is most significant. The habit of philosophy, the discipline that the love of wisdom classically developed, was a sense of perspective, a heuristic view of the whole. Naturally "the whole" has changed, as we have learned more about the universe and ourselves. But we human beings remain creatures primed to map the whole. In Plato's phrase, we want nothing less than to become as much like God as possible. As Aquinas saw, we are capable of becoming and making all things, because we have minds proportioned to whatever can exist. The love of learning activates this proportion, in the process showing us why each significant insight has a nisus to elevate us toward an overview of the whole. From the inside, as an inevitable byproduct of understanding, we begin to see the connections among all the beings of creation, the many-sided links. The love of wisdom is less interested in the particulars of such links than in the phenomenon of linkage itself. The more we free our students to explore problems that fascinate them, the more likely we are to develop minds that know for themselves that one can start anywhere in creation and soon find everything else implied.

Consider the student interested in music. Would it be difficult to demonstrate the relevance of physics (acoustics), mathematics (mensuration), history (the evolution of instruments), biology (how sound is received and processed), psychology (why music soothes the savage breast), sociology (how those who write the pop tunes shape the ethos), or theology (why Augustine said that those who sing pray twice) to the study of music? Could one not easily sketch a program through which a well motivated, bright, freed student might discover the universe of ideas and relations reticulating from music? I'm sure the answer is yes, though of course the ideal would be to have advice from specialists in the several areas I indicated on what would be the best way to move to the physical, mathematic, historical and other correlations.

At any rate, my main hope is to encourage readers to think creatively about honors education (the preparation of the best and the brightest) and to trust in the powers of the mind erotic for learning. When learning becomes beautiful, the fair maid or lad luring the student on, it is virtually bound to succeed. At that point our job as educators is simply to ease its passage and indicate the better problems or topics it ought to pursue.

All things exit into mystery, the venerable tag has it. Coined by an educated person, a person schooled in the dynamics and limitations of the human spirit, the tag reenforces what our honors curricula ought to target. We should feel free to aim at nothing less than the full sweep of being, all the fellow citizens with whom we share the universe, all the too-fullness, the pleroma, into which our sense of their sweep recedes. Grouped by their natural kinds and the times at which they emerged, they ask us for appreciation and cooperation. Berry's picture of the human species serving as the consciousness of the universe, or at least of the earth, may seem a poetic conceit, but it has some science and much philosophy to recommend it. The limits of the world's ability to appreciate its extent, depth, variety, and meaning are the limits of our human imagination, language, and contemplation. God and the angels don't need this physical world. We human beings, who for the psalmist are only slightly less than the angels, are the beings who need the physical world and have the most visceral urge to serve its prospering. If we can send out honors graduates who understand the earth, love it, and know how to serve its growth in self-consciousness and self-directedness, we shall have made an enormous contribution to the twenty-first century.

IX

AUTHORITY AND RESPONSIBILITY IN THE CLASSROOM

Whence do we professors of religion draw the audacity to speak about God and ultimate reality, about holiness and sacrifice, about the thoughts and actions that the majority of human beings, throughout history, have considered the staff of life? What is our responsibility to those we would initiate into the scholarly side of such mysteries, and how can we best fulfill it? Dare we expose our own passion for the glimpses of the divine that women and men have strewn throughout history? Dare we expose the doubts we have suffered, the times when we have wondered whether homo religiosus isn't mainly a fraud? What, in a word, is realistic in professing religion, in trying to communicate the yield of religious studies, in leading bands of students into the wilds of Scripture and Dharma and Tao? These are the vinous questions that have danced before me, when I have fortified myself for this chapter.

1. Authority

The college teacher who had the most lasting influence upon me was a wonderful professor of philosophy who brought the love of wisdom alive. In later years, when I had left the circle of her students and become her friend, she traveled under the nickname "Aristotle," like a don from a Dorothy Sayers mystery about an Oxford women's college. The nickname was ironic, since the syllogism was her students' nemesis. Yet it was also fitting, because she believed with all her heart that all people by nature desire to know, and that ultimate knowledge, metaphysics, treats of God, than whom there is nothing more intimate or ultimate.

"Aristotle" taught me, by her life more than her lectures, that the insight that finds intelligibility in phantasms moves in the traces of the thought that thinks itself--in the traces of the Being in whom to think and to exist coincide. Without so much as a nod to revealed religion, her deportment in the classroom was consummately devout. She worshiped at the shrine of the desire to know, that pure desire that Bernard Lonergan has made the key to the human vocation.

Strange, the uses that memory makes of one's school days. What remains a permanent encouragement, and what sloughs off into mere nostalgia, has little to do with the grades one received, the worries one mastered, even the books one read dutifully. What remains is the example of a person clearly committed to the love of wisdom. What remains is the gratitude one felt when a class occasioned one's own commitment to the spiritual life, the life of mind, heart, soul, and strength ecstatic for the beauty of the really real, the truly good.

My mentor in the classroom, "Aristotle," clarified my intellectual vocation, for which I shall stand forever in her debt. The mentors who formed me through their writings, such as Lonergan, are no less precious, having fed my soul the way the angel fed Elijah in the wilderness. Yet, without "Aristotle," I would not have been susceptible. I became a teacher because I wanted to make other people susceptible to genius. I became a teacher because I wanted to open others to the possibility of being taken outside themselves, for a glimpse of the really real, the truly holy. With junior high school students, high school students, and college undergraduates, I have plied my trade more than 30 years. Yet each Fall I begin with the jitters, dimly aware that this trade is audacious. By what authority can I presume to lead students into learning, the exploration of a wider reality, the traditions about wisdom and God? Certainly no degree, no credential, no advancement in academic rank supplies such authority. Nothing merely formal or extrinsic can. I get the jitters each Fall because I intuit, in familiar fear and trembling, that the only intrinsic authority is the Socratic one: knowing that one does not know, combined with an unrestrainable confession that one still yearns to know, with every fiber of one's being. This nescience, and the brute fact that I still yearn, have become my ground zero, that beyond which I cannot, and need not, go. I don't know the slightest portion of what there is to know, despite the hundreds of books I have read and the thousands of hours I have thought hard. Yet I am still in love, head over heels, with the prospect of knowing--of one day seeing face to face.

These fumblings with the roots, the existential foundations, of the teacher's authority now seem to me gnomic to the point of presocraticism. They remind me that I began with philosophical studies and only moved into religious studies when circumstance made religion the better raw material on which to work my craft. Philosophy having so frequently become verbalism, and the only paying job having appeared in a department of religion, I emigrated to religious studies, with an ease, a sense of homecoming, that then felt obvious but now feels remarkable.

Religious studies were more interested in the mysteries, the wisdoms, toward which I had long been oriented, though of course not simply so. What theologians told me was the dialectic of sin and grace operated in religious studies as well as philosophy, and to many peculiar effects. For there were scholars of religion, as well as philosophers, who declared the ultimate mysteries off-limits. There were professors of religion, as well as professors of epistemology, whose nescience was the vacuum I thought all sane people naturally abhorred. So it took me a while to find my bearings in religious studies and clarify just what existential authority entailed in my new classrooms. I finally decided it entailed exactly what it had entailed when I reverenced "Aristotle" and Bernard Lonergan, but I realized many would consider this position heterodox. For them mastering historical or ideational details was the ground of professorial authority. Aspiring to sit alongside physical or social scientists without having to blush, they threw empiricist elbows right and left. I was so busy ducking that I had no time to revere them.

And, on investigation, I found that their students also did not revere them, frequently did not even respect them. For their students intuited that they were more in flight from the mysteries of ultimate reality than in passionate pursuit. So their students found their professing of religion anomalous, if not hypocritical. More sophisticated than such students, and old enough not to judge precipitously, I was loathe to brand anyone hypocritical, yet I could not fail to take a lesson. Along the negative route, reading the entrails of failed ventures, I reinforced my conviction that in the spiritual disciplines, the Geisteswissenschaften, the passionate commitment of the teacher to the elusive truth being pursued is the crux of educational authority. If the teacher presents herself or himself as a seeker, in all rigor and humility, then the quest is rightly framed. If the teacher brackets intellectual passion, the pure desire to know, then the quest is lamed, halted, blinded-- defective from the outset. Certainly it is good for the teacher to know many things, to be well-read, disciplined, and exact. Certainly it is good for the teacher to be critical, acutely and obviously aware of the omnirelevance of suspicion. Yet neither scholarly familiarity nor critical acuity can hoist the full load. Both are necessary yet neither is sufficient. To meet the full conditions of exemplary teaching, the kind that would be memorable 30 years after and might turn a life around, one has to show oneself a lover of what one is pursuing, a devotee of the mysteries responsible for religion.

So, in my no doubt idiosyncratic view, the authority best equipping the teacher of religious studies is mystagogic. In all sobriety, one has to love and face every day the incommensurability of the subject matter one is trying to expose. Ironically, amusingly, this is the stance most akin to the teachers that religious people themselves have most revered. For it has not been the dusty scholastics, the doctrinaire academicians, who have fired the human spirit down the ages. It has been the teachers whose words overflowed from their own love of the divine mysteries, the teachers who gave instruction, by example as much as word, because they had no choice, because they could not do otherwise. They were the ones who had the words of eternal life, unforgettable and transforming. Those who lived off their words, writing commentaries and proffering glosses, were dangerous as well as necessary.

2. Responsibility

In Eric Voegelin's wonderful essay, "Reason: The Classic Experience" (available in his Anamnesis [Notre Dame: University of Notre Dame Press, 1978]), one finds a phenomenology of the search for the Beyond, and the luring by the Beyond, that makes the love of wisdom mystagogic. In Voegelin's exegesis of the capital finding of Plato and Aristotle, the dynamics of human intelligence move the seeker to the realization that what is sought can never be mastered. The best one can do is draw forth from one's engagement with the mysterious sought mythopoeic symbols that suggest the divinity and formative power that emerge in the seeking. It is baffling, if not humiliating, to find oneself so unequal to the task of mastering the movements constituting one's very spiritual life, yet one is consoled because such movements are more meaningful than anything else one has ever experienced. If busy, pragmatic, or empiricist people find one's consolation useless, so much the worse for them. In the leisure that is the basis for healing culture, one takes to heart the primacy of this contemplative life. And, ever after, one knows that one's primary responsibility is to keep faith with the experiential mystery that ordered one's soul and bid fair to order any others willing to attend and abide.

So, the main responsibility I see weighing on the teacher of religious studies is to become an habitue of the meditative disciplines that keep alive both the crux of what those seeking and being lured by the Beyond have come upon and what shapes the human spirit toward right order. Become such an habitue, the teacher of religious studies knows a source of stability that might keep her or him from the various imbalances, the various disorders, that threaten the sound study of religion. It is useful, of course, to add to this pneumatic differentiation, this existential clarification of the directedness of human consciousness, the several noetic differentiations that can separate and, ideally, integrate the philosophical, historical, comparative, social scientific, and other dimensions of human religiosity. It is useful, as well, to study challenges to a reading of human consciousness such as Voegelin's or Lonergan's. But the key task, for those who would be responsible, is to make the movement toward and being drawn by the Beyond that forms human consciousness central in one's assessment of the dynamics of the history of religion, including the dynamics of teaching religion critically.

Let me try to be more concrete. When I enter a classroom filled with students embarking on an

109

introduction to the world religions, I do well to ask myself what is the bottom line, the thing whose attainment will make the course a success and whose missing will make it a failure. You know how Father Guido Sarducci has answered this question. The bottom line is what one will recall ten years after graduating, and teachers would do everyone a favor if they would agree to form a "five minute university" that would dispense with the folderol and hand over the gist of each course. For economics, Sarducci has suggested, the gist might be, "The Law of Supply and Demand." For introductory Spanish, it might be, "Como esta usted?". The humor in the proposal eases our way into the poignant remainder or aftermath: What, in fact, is the heart of the matter? How, indeed, do we both separate the wheat from the chaff and ward off the atrophy of memory?

What, in fact, is the heart of the matter in a course in world religions--or, for that matter, virtually any other course in the religious studies curriculum? After one has exposed the students to a slice of the immense corpus of information, analysis, and evaluation, what should have riveted their souls? I believe that what should have riveted their souls is the unique creativity human beings have drawn from their quest to know the foundations of their world. I believe that a teacher's most personal responsibility is to have made it plain that the spiritual movements from which the great variety of human cultures has arisen are a never-failing source of wonder, significance, humility, and consolation.

Does this imply that teachers of religious studies can neglect the significance of the economy with which a given religious complex was entwined, or its prior history and tradition, or the psychotherapeutic aspects of the rituals and symbols it fashioned? Not at all. The clarifications of human order available in analysis of the constitutive movements of the human spirit make it plain that all the consequences of human embodiment must receive their due. Yet what empowers these consequences is human spirituality--human knowing and loving to the point of pilgrimage unto the Beyond. What makes how human beings have gotten their food or narrated their origins relevant to their present doctrines and ceremonies is the horizon they don't share with the lower animals, the horizon that condemns and blesses them to contend with the whole, the ground, the ultimacy of themselves and the rest of reality.

Another way of saying this is that the pedagogical finality of any course in religious studies that I can fully endorse is the students' becoming aware of what it means to be human in a religious mode. At another time, in another place, I might pursue the argument that one cannot be fully human apart from some involvement with religious modes, but sufficient for this day is the burden of explaining my sense of the pedagogical telos to which professors of religious studies ideally are responsible and faithful. For while one could say that any course in the humanities might set itself the grand, if not grandiose, goal of exposing its students to the wonders of their human makeup, it remains the peculiar advantage and responsibility of courses in religious studies to rivet such an exposure onto the most ultimate dynamics, which I believe to be mystagogic. Accidentally, teachers of history or literature may deal with the noetic and pneumatic differentiations that reveal the cognitive and affective aspects of human beings' pursuit of the Beyond and drawing by the Beyond. Ex professo, however, the teachers of religious studies that I would canonize display the dynamics of the depths of human consciousness as the constant source of culture and humanity and so the constant rationale for human religiosity, whether genuine or debased.

In acknowledging that human religiosity can be debased as well as genuine, I am of course opening the door to studies of religion that are critical in the sense of negative in their final evaluation of the practices, and perhaps also the beliefs, that have preoccupied many religious people and traditions throughout history. I myself do not finally assess the world religions as more harmful than beneficial, but it is not hard to see why others disagree, though how useful the whole matter of the humanity or inhumanity of the religions finally turns out to be is quite questionable. My greater interest is the criticism built into the very dynamics that Voegelin and Lonergan have emphasized. Willy-nilly, we use these dynamics whenever we move to judgment and evaluation, so they themselves furnish the best criteria for what is authentically human, or authentically religious, and what is not. Once again, on another occasion it might

111

be profitable to take up the problem that any precisely theological position, indebted to a particular set of scriptures and traditions, might find with the prospect of making our spiritual movement toward the Beyond the criterion of authentic humanity. For present purposes, however, it seems wise to adapt Occam's razor and say that theological difficulties are not to be multiplied without necessity.

If I have made it clear that the puzzling business of discovering what makes human beings human is peculiarly appropriate to courses in religious studies, peculiarly a responsibility of teachers of religious studies, I shall be more than satisfied. And if I have convinced even one reader that the roots of this peculiar appropriateness are the overlaps between the Beyond inalienable to human consciousness and the divinities or nirvanas or Taos so beloved by the world religions, I shall be positively exultant. Either way, I can only hope that when teachers of religious studies consider their basic responsibilities, they recognize the primacy of playing true to the movements in their own souls that cause them to keep questioning, to the point of confronting the mysterious Beyond.

3.   Further Questions

Having touched on the issues of authority and responsibility in the classroom, let me conclude by taking up the three further matters I mentioned at the outset: our own passion for the divine, our doubts about homo religiosus, and what are realistic expectations.

First, dare we expose our own passion for the glimpses of the divine that women and men have strewn throughout history? Why not? Presumably we would not deny the proposition that we are as human as the students in front of us or the historical figures we treat. Presumably we would not exempt ourselves from the searches and lurings, the seductions and disappointments, regular for people who want to know ultimate reality. But if this is so, we should have no difficulty confessing the times and ways that the recurrent human passion for God, the recurrent human desire to know beyond particulars, to know and feel and love to the depths, seized our own spirits. Naturally, we would be wise to avoid anything approaching the style of True Confessions, anything overly dramatic or

112

self-exalting. Preferably, our speech will be critical as well as enthusiastic, restrained as well as poetic. But, should we feel so moved, there is nothing wrong with our admitting the times when our own mouths were stopped, our own hearts missed a beat, because our spirits went rapt over a glimpse of beauty, or coruscant meaning, or a darkness that made sense of nothingness. Equally, there is nothing wrong with our admitting that a text of Plato, or an Upanishad, or a gospel scene, or a Hasidic tune, or a Confucian proverb once struck us so forcefully that our awareness jumped a notch and we've never been quite the same since.

Here I am distinguishing implicitly between exposing one's passion for the heart of religious experiences and lobbying for a given religious tradition or orthodoxy. If one is to remain in the realm of religious studies, in contrast to theological studies, such lobbying is not appropriate. Completely appropriate, in my view, is a perduring enthusiasm for the movements that other human beings have claimed made them most human, and that we ourselves have access to if we are willing to study such claims contemplatively. Just as historians are usually better teachers when they are enthusiastic about their period, or art critics are usually better teachers when they communicate their love of certain kinds of beauty, so teachers dealing with religion usually profit from a passion for the Beyond, or the Within, or the Center, or the whatever else they sense is the most significant mover of human beings.

But, second, what about the negative aspects of our studies in the world religions? Dare we expose the doubts we have suffered, the times when we have wondered whether homo religiosus isn't a fraud? Once again, why not? If what we are studying is significantly ourselves--a human nature we know and cherish from within--then it is wholly legitimate to expose the doubts that the spiritual movement quickening human beings' pursuit of ultimate meaning regularly raise. Here the distinction most pertinent is between the products of religious endeavor and the source of that endeavor. Thus, we should distinguish between (a) doubting the beauty, truth, or wholesomeness of many of the results of human beings' religious activities throughout the ages and (b) doubting the reality or worth of the movement toward the Beyond, and the drawing by the Beyond, that arguably constitutes our ineluctable impulse toward fuller humanity. To doubt the latter would be to take a hatchet to our very makeup, and to involve ourselves in self-contradiction. If we say that we have no passion to move beyond, we say so in virtue of the spiritual movements involved in making such a judgment, and so we affirm substantially what we are denying verbally. In fact, the most benign, and often the most accurate, interpretation of the radical doubts to which the hermeneutic of suspicion seems to have led some eminent academicians is that they glimpsed the dark mysteriousness into which the truly foundational search leads and either were frightened by this mysteriousness or realized they would never have words to name it adequately.

Third, what is realistic in professing religion, in trying to communicate the yield of religious studies, in leading bands of students into the wilds of Scripture and Dharma and Tao? What can one reasonably hope to achieve? This is the question that best reveals the consolations of the phenomenology of spiritual movement on which I've depended. We can reasonably hope to achieve moments of recognition, whether few or many, that bring a look of intrigue, or startlement, or smiling puzzlement, or even radiant joy to the faces in front of us. Naturally, much of what we achieve is out of our hands. I am sure that Lonergan had just come back from class when he wrote his wonderfully sardonic line, "Insight is the act that occurs frequently among the intelligent and rarely among the stupid." Similarly, agreement to mystagogy is the act that occurs frequently among the contemplative and rarely among the extraverted, the distracted, the superficial. Still, even the superficial have depths and dynamics inviting them toward transcendence, however unaware they may be.

Sometimes I think that the greatest service of introductory courses in metaphysics and world religions is the bafflement they can create. For the first time, in many cases, students are asked to consider the Beyond and the Beginning, not just as terms translated from a catechism but as terms correlated with experiential spiritual movements, as terms struggling to name orientations and foundations of consciousness. If we can make "God" or "Suchness" or the "Tao" ciphers for experiential gropings after order and ultimate meaning, experiential responses to stirrings in people's spirits, then we can make someone aware of the specific difference constituting his or her human species. We humans are the beings who want to know, and whose wanting to know can become the love of their lives. We are also the beings who only frustrate their wanting to know and love unrestrictedly at the price of a significant, perhaps a damning, loss of their humanity.

I believe it is quite realistic to think that approaching religious studies mystagogically will gain one wrinkled brows, and to hope that some of the minds behind those wrinkled brows will be changed by the realization that the world just may be much richer than what eye can see, ear can hear, it can enter the human heart to conceive. I further believe that when we correlate such an expectation with an authority and responsibility rooted in what the spiritual movements of the religious traditions have suggested is the crux of being human, we achieve a satisfying integrity. Our teaching professes nothing we cannot stand by, nothing we cannot deliver. Taking our stand on the dynamics of the movement toward the Beyond justifies a first job description of simply helping students discover both what it means to be human and how mysterious and absorbing such meaning can be.

Moreover, this job description meshes us with the interests and passions and achievements of the religious figures who have bequeathed us so much of our present inventory of human possibilities. The shamans and yogins, prophets and sages, teachers and priests, mystics and charismatics who decorate the pages of the history of religion comprise a great illustration of the discovery that becoming fully human entails moving beyond present attainments, moving toward the silence and darkness that alone adequately suggest the fullness and mystery in which we are immersed. I count it a great privilege to work at communicating appreciations such as these, and I hope that my fellow professors will continue to count it the same.

X

CONCLUSION: THE GOOD ALLIANCE

We have reflected on feminist consciousness, the
place of feminist perspectives in the curricula of
religious studies departments, the impact of feminist
thought on the Christian reconception of God, the
experience of women in the Christian church, the story
of world religions as a whole, and such educational
matters as the place of values in the general
curriculum, the place of values in the education of
honors students, and how teachers of religious studies
ought to regard the authority and responsibility they
exercise in the classroom. It is time to cast a
retrospective eye on the relations among feminism,
religion, and education, in an effort to seal their
complementarity into the partnership of a good
alliance.

To put the matter baldly, I might say that there
will be no optimal alliance unless feminists, people of
faith, and educators can agree that religion is the
substance of the good life and that feminism and
education are privileged ways of expressing religion.
No doubt this thesis will outrage many feminists and
educators, but it is what I find when I examine the
convictions undergirding my own career as an educator
who has specialized in religious studies and has
developed feminist sympathies. Of course, I do not
want this thesis to be taken simplemindedly. Perhaps
the first step on the way to showing how it might not
be would be to define the sense of religion with which
I am working.

The religion I have in mind is not the product of
any single faith. It is also not Christianity,

conceived as either the fulfillment of all religious, or all human, aspiration or as a perfect entity dictated by God. Rather, the religion I have in mind is the outreach of the human mind and heart toward the Beyond of divinity--of the transcendent holiness that we hope in our bones is the justification of our otherwise wretched lives. I believe that this holy divinity is implied in each movement of the human spirit toward truth and goodness, in each human act of understanding and love. The mystery onto which our most human operations open is the mystery of God--that is my most basic conviction. One cannot be human apart from this mystery, so "humanity" and "divinity" are correlative terms.

Certainly, God is not confined by human beings. God did not have to create a world, and God did not need limited incarnate spirits such as we to fulfill the divine existence. But, after the fact of creation, human beings are bound to think of God as the fulfillment of their best intuitions, and divinity is "bound" to reveal itself in incarnational ways: symbols, analogies, the lives of holy men and women who have set their hearts on a goodness they can feel but cannot understand. This being "bound" is what "religion" is all about, both etymologically and analytically. Human beings are naturally religious because by nature we want to deal with a holy Whole that might explain, justify, and redeem our lives. So the religion in which I am most interested overlaps with the effort to become a mature human being. Regardless of what name a person gives herself, if she is struggling to become wise and good, she is involved with the mysteriousness that I call "God."

In fact, I interpret this mysteriousness in virtue of my Christian faith. In fact, I have never outgrown the cradle Catholicism that considers the human spirit to be naturally Christian and thinks that the divine mystery is the fulfillment of every good thing for which the human heart longs. The life, death, and resurrection of Jesus of Nazareth have been my prime interpreters of the optimal human life, and I do not blush to say that I have found nothing to match this Christian hermeneutic for depth or beauty. But I also think that one ought to be able to talk with any serious person about the mystery that solicits attention on every side of human existence. As well, I think that many people who would never darken the door of a church, or a synagogue, or a mosque are actually very religious. My God is not a positivist, bound to the rules of evidence developed by a particular religious community. My God is the far side of every ardent human being's reach for love, for understanding, for a cause worth the sacrifice of life itself.

To my mind, Jesus of Nazareth discloses an invitation that God has placed in all human hearts. Wherever there is a pulse of desire for something pure and wholly good, the God that Jesus called "Abba" is present, dealing with the person in question like a loving parent. Conservative Christians may discount such an analysis as diluting the message of the gospel. In my view, such an analysis is much more faithful to Christ than any reading that limits salvation to institutional Christianity, because such an analysis follows Jesus's own conviction that God treats all of us like the father of the prodigal son we find in Luke 15.

It follows, then, that I subordinate feminism and education to religion because I see religion as the intercourse with divine mystery that makes human beings what they are called to be, while I see feminism and education as potent ways of articulating or nurturing people's intercourse with divine mystery. Only the divine mystery itself is absolute. To set anything else in the place of the incomprehensible divine mystery is to commit idolatry--to settle for the part rather than the whole. Some feminists seem to commit idolatry in this way, making their political or ideological cause an absolute. To my mind that is folly--a course of action or thought bound to be disappointing. When the Bible said that we should not put our trust in princes, it certainly implied that we also should not put our trust in princesses. The grass withers, the flower fades--only the Word of the Lord endures. Ideology is a poor substitute for genuine, mystagogic religion. In the presence of the living mystery of God, of the sovereign darkness and silence that cannot yield to human manipulation because it is aboriginal and they are derivative, all ideology-- Marxist, feminist, Muslim, liberal, Christian (the reification of Christian dogma), or other--seems like cant. The revelation of Christ is that no one has ever seen God. The only-begotten Son who is in the bosom of the Father is a Logos whom not even the flesh of Jesus renders into graspable form.

Truly higher education is that which acknowledges the primacy and permeation of the divine mystery, if only in its forms of the Beginning and Beyond, and which tries to educe young people's capacities for living full lives in the light of human beings' condemnation to not knowing the full import of their situation. I see education as the best way to help the next generation realize the potential latent in its embodied spirituality. But I would never confuse what education may accomplish with the gist of being human, because it is plain that many people who do badly in school turn out to be especially wise or holy.

Education, like feminism and ecclesiology, always runs the risk of losing the spirit, the original vision, among the letters. The laws and regulations and customs that organizations require need not block out the priority of the divine mystery, but regularly they attempt to do so. Thus I find a kinship among the ideological posturings of doctrinaire feminists, educational bureaucrats, and many representatives of the hierarchical church. They may once have had an original, creative spirit (an impulse from the divine Spirit), but administration, or habituation, or rhetoric, or the demons of self-righteousness have eroded it. So they find it necessary to intone formulas, to incant ritualistic runes, as shields against not only the darkness of chaos and fearsome failure but also the darkness of divinity, which always refuses to deliver itself into human understanding.

Not to put too fine a point on it, I find no salvation in either feminism or education. Puffed up into reasons for a human being to be, they become all air and no substance. The only substance I have found dependable is the divine mystery that we best intuit and taste when we stumble into love. In love, we know what we have been made for. In love, we are sure that the world has had some purpose, our lives have not been useless passions. God is the security of such love, the mysterious guarantee that we have not been idiotic to risk our souls on what eye cannot see, ear cannot hear, it cannot enter the human heart to conceive or secure. The order among feminism, religion, and education is therefore plain. Two are servants and one is master. Two derive from a vision or mystical experience of the holy whole and one is that vision or experience, however tattered and inadequate. Unless this ratio holds, one has perversion—the disorder of the means trying to establish itself as the end.

Religious Appreciations of Feminism and Education

Granted a proper order among the three partners to the coalition that I am proposing, what ought one to think about the potential of feminism and education? First, I believe that one ought to think that their potential is great, and that they will best actualize their potential by staying faithful to their own germinal instincts.

The germinal instinct that I find at the origins of feminism stresses that the humanity of women is the equal of the humanity of men. From this core intuition flow all the positions about women's rights in the workplace, in the home, in the churches, in the universities, among the united nations. When feminists stick to their conviction that women are as human as men, many problems dissolve conceptually if not practically. When it comes to equal pay for equal work, there is no conceptual problem—because male and female workers stand on the same footing. When it comes to equal access to authority and responsibility—whether in the classroom, or the corporate boardroom, or the corridors of government, or the ministries of the religious bodies—once again there is no conceptual problem, because nothing sexual gives a candidate an intrinsic advantage. Even such troubled matters as abortion clarify greatly: women do not have unique rights, nor do men. Both have contributed half the genetic endowment, so both start their discussions as equally essential to the processes of procreation and parenting.

The religion that I want to encourage takes this core feminist intuition and secures it in the divine mystery. When women or men are passionately committed to the equality of the sexes, they often glimpse the limits of human beings' ability to secure justice and so are primed to appreciate how human existence lives and moves and has its being within something much greater. By keeping faith with their commitment to the equality of the sexes, feminists can grow wonderfully mature. They can come to realize both the necessity and the futility of human efforts to secure justice. And that, in turn, can make them religious in the way

that I find most attractive: people humbled by the
mysteriousness of the condition into which they have
been cast, people primed for reflection, contemplation,
worship and self-sacrifice.

The core intuition on which higher education
depends is that learning brings a quantum leap in
people's humanity. Because of the central place that
our minds hold in our lives, the development of our
minds is bound to influence our whole lives. The
traditional imagery for education, implied in the
etymology of the term, is that teachers "lead out" the
potential of their students. Similar is the Platonic
imagery of mid-wifery. Teachers do not create the
potential for learning. They do their best work when
they stimulate the innate capacities of their students
and get out of their students' way.

From a religious perspective, stimulating
students' innate capacities is bound to move them
toward a confrontation with the mysteriousness of the
human condition. Consequently, it is bound to make the
realities, if not the language, of salvation and
redemption pertinent. Why is it that human beings
suffer so much pain? What is the source of the
injustice and cruelty that go beyond the caprices of
nature and must be laid at our own species' door? How
might we overcome such injustice and cruelty? Is it
possible to redesign the human race, so that it might
escape from its vicious cycles of violence and
retaliation?

Any teacher of religion worth her or his salt
knows how to let questions such as these emerge from
intellectual inquiries that begin with apparently
innocuous problems such as disparities in income or
patterns in the nations' history of war. Any teacher
mystagogic the way that I would like teachers to be
also knows how to insist that these bedrock questions
cannot be answered propositionally. They are modes of
inquiry that take the inquirer toward the
mysteriousness of the human condition, toward the
divinity that is ingredient in our makeup as people who
raise questions about their basic condition. Any
answers that come from letting them carry one into the
divine mystery first occur as colorations of the
inquirer's soul and then express themselves
symbolically, sacramentally, in stories pivoted on

wonders such as crucifixion or rites consecrating elements such as bread and wine.

Second, from my religious perspective feminism and education are natural modes in which people's basic search for meaning can express itself well because both entities have such a profound hold on the human personality. If we use feminism to spotlight the matter of sexuality, we cast light on something as intimate and inalienable as our own bodies. We exist in sexed bodies and this fact colors everything that we think and do. If we use education to spotlight the matter of intellectual maturation, we cast light on how we think, what ties our thought has to our bodies and our cultures, how what we think leads us to spend our money and our love. Women think "mind-bodily," and so do men (see William Poteat"s Polanyian Meditations [Durham, NC: Duke University Press, 1985]). Neither women nor men are determined by their sex to arrive at certain intellectual positions, but both women and men bring sexual baggage to education.

Naturally enough, feminists have looked to education as a prime way of getting out their message and saving the next generation from the sexist deformations perpetrated in the past. Equally naturally, alert educators have dealt with sexuality in their work as literary critics, historians, cultural anthropologists, and the like. It is easy to conceive of feminists and educators as natural allies, though of course such a conception breaks down in many particular circumstances. Equally, it is easy to think of believers and educators as allies, though history tells us that the schools and the churches have often had tense relationships. Finally, it is easy for me to think of believers and feminists as allies, because I think that they need one another. Feminists show believers how unregenerate much of their behavior and thought has been concerning women, while believers show feminists the farther reaches of the questions they pursue and the inevitability of the human follies that raise the issue of salvation.

Inasmuch as enlightenment does not save us from folly, religion is bound to strike dispassionate people as the deepest of human ventures. The transformation of human nature that the various religious systems have attempted stands in history as the most stunning of cultural causes. When feminists attempt a new transformation of human nature, they work as believers trying to mediate salvation. When educators strive with might and main to remove ignorance and bring sweet reason to bear on all human affairs, they too work as believers trying to mediate salvation. Salvation--healing, rescue, recreation--is at the center of all the noble human enterprises that history records. Medicine and law, politics and art, even warfare and commerce have often been undertaken as efforts to so change the status quo, the prevailing state of affairs, that a new order might emerge. Wisdom would seem to lie in a moderate position that encourages people to summon up their salvational energies without letting them think that any purely human efforts will ever take them where they long to go.

If people committed to such primal causes as liberating human sexuality, and liberating the human mind, and liberating the human spirit by making it familiar with divine mystery should ever join forces, they would create a splendid alliance indeed. I have felt privileged to work at all three of these causes, and to reflect on their interactions. Much of the hope that gets me out of bed in the morning and allows me to sleep peacefully at night comes from the good people I have met on all three fronts. My best friends are those who share my own threefold allegiance. So I must conclude on an upbeat note: when I see feminists, educators, and people of religious faith realizing that their causes have a great deal to offer one another, I see the alliance that I want to work with for the rest of my years.